ANOTHER RUBBER EDEN

ANOTHER RUBBER EDEN

Vincent Quatroche

This book was printed in the United States of America.

Library of Congress Number 98-85979
ISBN (Hardcover) 0-7388-0015-5
ISBN (Softcover) 0-7388-0031-7

To order additional copies of this book, contact:
Xlibris Corporation
1-888-7-XLIBRIS
www.Xlibris.com

CONTENTS

OUTSIDE OF MY IMMEDIATE FAMILY (WIFE, KIDS, FOLKS, AND SISTERS) AND FEW DOZEN CLOSE AND LOYAL COLLEAGUES, LIFE LONG FRIENDS, BARTENDERS AND "OLD TIME USED TO BE'S" THE REST OF YOU SMART ASS BASTARDS CAN GO STRAIGHT TO HELL.

INSTRUCTIONS FOR UNDERSTANDING THIS POEM

Take line A and misread it.
The green tractor cast a shadow on the black top.
Insert the colors B & C into line D.
She was a blue swimming pool in the winter's morning sun.
Fold the imagery in lines F & G into a paper airplane
and sail into the waste basket.
"You know," he snarled, "Your daily intents could fit into
a small city's Sunday Leisure Time Section."
Lines L & M contain sarcasm, adjust attitude accordingly
to fit the defeatism in lines J & K.
Now your green tractor should be interlocked in the
        swimming
pool, along with that woman in the winter's morning sun.
Go back to the waste basket in line J. Fish out the imagery
and see if it flies any better. Then refer back to line A.
Now burn the basketball player's hands, while deep frying
french fries at four in the morning, bench him for a month.
Take the cryptic reference of lines EE & FF and line up with
the following irony. Reverend who advocates use of condoms
from the pulpit has police record for attempted rape.
Put him on the green tractor with that woman in the pool.
Now insert the basketball player's hands on the small cities
Leisure Time Sunday section in lines L & M.
Repeat lines H & I & J. Refer back to line A.

Time for the modern pedagogy gone awry.
Day Care teacher dressed as Care Bear beaten,
by Sixth Graders on Valentine's Day in West Virginia.
Now you should have the Reverend, Day Care Teacher and
the blue swimming pool in the winter's morning sun.
    (line F)
Make the green tractor red. (line B).
All personification, metaphor and meaning should be clear.
If not, refer back to line A.

Fall 1991

WINTER

In the factory
In the prison
In the winter
I am the factory
To the winter
In the prison.

I hear their stories at night
next to the booking desk.
The naked fear in her voice,
the resignation of her explanation.
Too young, too pretty, too much trouble again.
And she said she told the lady on the phone
that her kid is home alone.
But it's not like the movie, or being with
television cops who parole you with every commercial.

I walk by the trap at night
and give it a quick sideways glance.
It's between protective administrative isolation
and day care's "time out".

I talk softly in the little house.
So what else would you like to know?
I work in the factory.
I teach at the jail.
I need to get drunk
but never throw up in a pail.

Yes this is my natural face
no I didn't fall down
but my occasional lucidity
I did frequently quite successfully drown.

But don't swing into verse here
on my account.
It's just a factory
or a prison in the winter.

So wish for a cab.
and a fare to beat later

because beer break is over
the clock beats away on the wall
and your sentence is to have to look
for one good solid riff in
all this factory
all this winter.

Can I remember my dreams
in this winter of factories and prisons.
Do my time.

To record:
The ghost trailing full on the tail pipes
like a little kid trying to keep up.
The morning had an odd lot
certain puddles about the gutter holes
or mirrors dashing reflections in front
of cars like terrified cats thinking
"If only I could get to the other side."
Last night I drove home from the prison in a thick fog.
Each street light cut a cone going down
shafts that poured a dirty wet yellow
in funnels of light cut inverted into the blackness.

I watch the sky brighten each dawn
and once
heard the sound in a green room
while three metal vats hummed or chanted or groaned
in finely ground Polypropylene.
I could sing along, at least to that.

But I only heard it once.
You sing that factory.
So near the prison
in the winter.

I can't call you
out of the factory
so much like the prison
is the winter of our season.

To walk out in the dawn
I hear a heavy door swing open
here is your common release

some sort of parole
from winter in the factory.

I remember starting this in blackness
a silent icy blizzard of interment.
Now the dawn fire cries gulls
The sky is a blush broken vase of color.
I have gone from the darkness into the light.
Still winter and spring bicker over the factory
They long to dance, but struggle to let each
other lead or leave or arrive and the wind
howls one season's name and sky writes the other
 and in the confusion
there is this glorious donnybrook of light.

I will walk out today
into another ending.
I have made the transition
from a curious disfigured stranger to
that "pintaho" who used to work here,
that supposed "teacher" who thought himself
too good to work on Saturdays.
Now as the grey people scuffle past
mumbling in a foreign tongue
hissing glances at six a.m. to face
another ten hour day of tedium and drudgery.
I feel little save the distance approaching
rapidly between our lives.

This grey street will evaporate this afternoon.
My parking spot will open up forever.
Upon exiting the factory
my footsteps will not echo.
I leave nothing here
except a punched out time card
a brutal sweaty map tracing ordinary toil.

Today I vanish from their harsh world.
My simple March into April's escape
where I still hope to be able to dream
and try to remember my time.
In the prison
In the factory
of this winter.

                                       3/29/96

OF ORAL AND VISUAL

I wish I had been alive
when Pollock was slinging paint
swinging colors
in a hot dusty barn
August afternoons near Sagaponack.

Landscape steaming heat waves melting pigment
blazing marshes cat-tail explanation points.
Ripple current salt blue pools sending the sky
into a jealous furious rage of envy over tincture
exclusivity. Heat stroking a wild furnace of chaos
when nature crawls off the palette, to rage, seethe
hissing summer. To puncture the vision's depth of
field, split the infinitives and just spit it out:
WHITE COCKATOO with EYES IN THE HEAT
drunk on SCENT riding A GREYED RAINBOW.

That's what I must do with words now.
But you've got to get the picture.
See the shattered dancing picture.
If you don't see it.
If you don't see it.
Then I didn't do it.

Write in color.
If I could throw the verbal heat like a Koufax fastball.
Who could catch it?
Who would be able to tell the difference from a distance

between Sandy and Serling?
Who wrote in a twilight prose of black and white.
From memory. From incident.
In the PURPLE TESTAMENT with the 11th Airborne
        Division
Skytrooper Serling shot a Japanese soldier leading off third
base bottom half of World War, inning 2, 1945
at Rizal Stadium during street-to-street combat for Manila.

Years later in glacial Upstate New York winter afternoon.
I have one hallucination of him out the side door of
the garage in the neighbor's back yard.

He gestures in the driving snow to me.
Then a shuttering wink white-out wind gust
-I'm standing on the sidewalk of the Upper East Side

1955 city blizzard just outside of a bar.
I walk in the door from the blinding frozen light.
And there he's sitting at the bar in a thin black tie and
charcoal hounds tooth sports jacket with Edwardian collars
another freshly lit cigarette and parting the
veil of smoke he turns to regard me.
He grimaces slightly
beckoning me to interior shadows
titling his head on an angle says,

"Sit down, I've just had this idea for a story and
I need someone to tell it to."

                                        2/97

HER ROLL OF LOST PICTURES

So then his thunder was exposed as an endangered species.
Your brief downpour of words
soaked the situation to everyone's dissatisfaction.
They have this sure fleeting flash of
momentary light. Illumination to La Carte.
Sure shows everything up. You can count on it.
But only so far for tonight. (and of course there are
expressly no substitutions.)

Move this night like a set of negatives never exposed
within aperture. Seems the film just never became tightly
        enough
twisted in a circle about the housing.

Much was missed. Still no one had the guts or the smarts to
question the intent. . . . but near the end I seemed to over
hear some smug talk from somebody so very intent on making
a point to everyone's satisfaction.

Or was that barter: trade you your cross to bear for my axe
to grind: or Sure... you can remain the foremost expert in the
following category: most likely to be lost in translation.

I can't change the way you waste one of the last few good
days at the start of September (like you had lots).

Let's just try a small voice then saying, "if you have to
go, make the most of the season. Fall into October's arms
already ablaze intent upon."

And if you find you don't have anyone's name to call
when autumn's dream coat flashes some spectrum vivid;
remember how I once waited up for you call
while dropping plenty like the number of thunderstorms
left you could count on your
right hand after August.

9/97

THE RAIN ON THE TRAIN FALLS MOSTLY ON THE POOR.

Have you ever ridden the train from blackness
into the light?
Have you waited at the station in the cold pre-dawn shroud
of March straining to hear your next hallucination
shatter the reverberating stillness in increments
of approaching motion and steel?

The dizzy travelers upon the platform, puffy eyed with
interrupted sleep speaking softly in their native tongue.
The suspicious slanting eye glances of over-burdened
college students.
The relief you feel being so far away from them.
The children's faces aglow with flushed excitement and
a roughly roused dream veneer clinging about them
like an escaping steam pipe's ghost.
It's true.
Everyone gets on.

This time the shadows have escaped.
This time the shadows are on the scurry
like symphonic signatures of mad rushing movement.
It turns me this way and then another.
And all that matters this morning is the going.
The coach has gone from dark to light.

Now morning being born slides by the sides
an exotic dancer muttering woods in thistles,
in the whispers of the whistles, swaying figure 8's
belly dancing epistles about your coffee being too hot
to drink yet, but not too hot to drop in your lap.

The coach is this lonely woman with her two small kids.
I can catch a glimpse of her eyes in the slit of the space
between the seats and her eyes burn with this desperate
resignation over the recognition of all that time,
all that despair, all the years she would like to have back,
to know then, what she knows now.
That is, how brutally, how matter-of-fact, the common world
accepts and drains the pure warm light that pours out of her
dark eyes and into the porous, bottomless track-bed without
so much as a shrug of death's shoulders. So this morning, she
isn't telling any Brett Butler jokes, on this very early
morning journey to Grand Ma "Jennies" and I hear her voice,
three seats over telling her oldest, "Ya better be good
or we ain't gonna go on no more trains."

Ask me later about the sound of her voice.

4/95

HERE ARE THE BLUE PRINTS

I ran into her last Saturday Night there, bub,
in the bar just after midnight. I was lit in the
crowd, leaning on the bar, just pissing away what
was left of any youth that I hadn't yet managed to squander.
And she came up all blonde and young and I can never
remember her name, you knew her better than I did,
I suppose. And she looked a little tired maybe a
little blue and quiet, not quite the ecstatic,
elastic rubber motion laughing whirlwind who would
get drunk and bubbly as champagne freshly shot
out of the bottle, laughing and dancing with everyone.
No, tonight dammit she looked lonely and she
explained a little too quietly how she was just around
for the night and her date had stood her up in
another bar across town. So now she stood there talking
to me looking sad and beautiful and like just one good
reason to jump start her eyes just might get her going
again. And, of course, she asked about you, how you
were, where you were, why you weren't down here drinking
with me and how she would have loved to see you.

And what the hell was I supposed to say?
That you had begged off much earlier, with tax day being
shoved up your ass, so you could cough up the damage later,
and freshly canceled car insurance, just a little

forget-me-not by product of a late night binge last
winter with that nice polite State Trooper, and of
course divorce number two just getting started and all
this one wanted was your first male son and
most of your thirty year pension.
All I could do was think of you home by yourself, very
lonely, probably half in the bag, in that big friggin
house by yourself maybe jerking yourself off to try
and get to sleep and I looked at her young, soft
sad, little face with the big blue twenty-two year
old eyes and said, "oh, he's fine. Little headache
tonight, a lot of writing to do, you know him,
always working on something."

"Uh-huh" she mumbled and looked down the bar for
someone younger and better looking to hang with.
She wasn't even listening when I said, "Too bad
people like you never get together with the others like
you that really do need someone, not forever, just
tonight, in a cheap, quiet, decent little roadside motel
called, "The Shaded Lamplite" with a half a case of
beer, a little scotch, some decent reefer, a small cassette
deck, a brown bag of full of candles, beauty and beast
strawberry bubble bath and the firm belief that the
world will end at dawn.

                                                    4/96

WHISPERING WEEKS

Still Life Prose Photographs of the Last Few Months.

Shoulders wedged between two young women with long
brown hair in a blue pick up truck on an August afternoon.
Paradise perfect sky with young white slow crawling clouds.
Our wheels sliding down a long smooth hillside straddling
the worn warm blacktop's blue-grey ribbon. Everybody has
some wind in their hair and their shoulders all are bouncing
in time to the movement.

So that when the Serpents of the Sound swam in the distance
looping around all twisted feces brown I stood on the
bluffs without a camera. I'm thinking, "No one is going
to believe this."

Have I lost my pen down here at last?
I've been dreaming about the dark woman again.
At dawn I'm waking, shaking my head, reverberating over
images too rich for my hand. Where was the page for all
this? I will need your help. Here. Reach.
Maybe you can hold this ink shrouded silhouette steady.
The features of her face lost in shadow from which behind
burns the red and blue beer neon beacon screen windows
fanning out from it all like a fine steel spider's web.
I keep getting these phone calls from dreams.
I answer the answer, but there is only silence.
No voice ever speaks and then they always hang up.

I was in the water up to my neck
looking back towards the shoreline.
I'm watching the milky flesh of two young naked girls
just entering the water. Dark brown tufts of pubic
triangles and taut center pink rubber ball breasts
approach into the waves in striding rhythm.
They are laughing as the lake swallows them slowly up.

She refuses to be lost in the crowd.
The more people in the theater the stronger
I can feel her presence in the unspeakable music.
The audience can neither see nor hear any of this.
I fail to recognize my place with them.
I can feel everything they can't.
The music score is impossible to describe.

Concussions of irony, sadness, promise, meaning
cascade and echo all over the huge hall.
I'm dreaming of the dark woman again.
I can't stop it. She is coming into all this.

Near the end of the performance
as the audience filed out looking disappointed
I stood in an aisle aware of what was next.
A white curtain parted up on the stage and
she appeared with her thick dark hair swept up
upon her head; she was smiling at me.
I'm dreaming about the dark woman again.

That sky has turned that funny color, that odd shade.
Not really orange. Saying pink would be too easy.
Diffused blue would be letting everybody off too easy.
C'mon big boy say something abstract.

Later, that night, we were all drinking beer in
their room. Tigger got up to go to the bathroom.

The moment she shut the door behind her I dove between
Lucy's legs and began to work her long cotton skirt
upwards with my head while using my tongue in a long
slow upward motion hanging a slight right angle at
her kneecaps toward the flanks and the soft inner
thigh. She wasn't wearing underwear. But then again,
she didn't need any.

7/95-9/95

DREAM FATIGUE

When he awoke that morning he felt
as if he had been sleeping like an
oil pan with a cross-threaded reservoir plug
and all night leaking.

Recalled images had this veil upon them
Only fragments of scenes were visible.
A beautiful young girl naked on the beach.
The kiss interrupted by the appearance of
a foolish puffy-faced rival with a greasy
wavy pompadour. The ensuing argument.
The darkening sky over a fading shoreline.
Distant thunder replaced by a chewing sound.
The hand of someone attempting to write with
an eraser pencil. The shadow trail of words.
A set of ears on the silence. Pictures of places
in the past that no longer existed. Her green patio.
A screened-in tree house on a July evening.
The sound of zipper being yanked down. The lights
from the darkened frame of the house glowing like
lanterns covered with Vaseline. Eyes opening in
the leaves. Whispers hissing from the shadows.
The sky gradually peeling back a thin light blue
illumination like a dancer slowly hiking up her
skirt. The smell of the pillow. A knocking at the
door.

12/2/94

V.J.Q. THE 1ST

Back from a gig-
Small house. Good check.
Got to have that money up front.
Six hours in the car out of nine.
It rained and the road was twisted
in glistening black ribbons
that bound your back up in knots.
Now I'm safe and sound lit pumpkin content
looking at the orange glow of the marigold
blossoms from my garden cut and assembled in pickle jars.

And I'm thinking of you.
You were the musician. The drummer. The back beat.
A member in the SUFFOLK SERENADERS.
You, asleep in the back seat of the car on the way
home from an engagement just after Christmas
that year. A drunk in the other lane crossed
the double line and ran the band's car off the road.

You never regained consciousness.
You lingered in the hospital
until the afternoon of New Year's day of 1939.
You died and left a widow called Dottie
who smoked Camels, who knew you screwed around
on the side and five kids, all under the age of
sixteen for her to raise by herself.

Your oldest son became an Artist.
His son a Poet.
Your son has told me stories about you.
The first Vincent James.
You were the grandfather I never met.
It is difficult to imagine you as I'm
older now than you ever grew.
Sometimes on nights like these when I've escaped your fate I
       think about it.
I think that the trio of us could have been
something in a room; I wonder if we'll get the chance to find
       out in eternity.

Hey Vince,
the beer is cold tonight at my house.
White foam in a golden glow.
Maybe a little like it might have been in another glass in
       Southampton in 1923.
And on nights like this, at this hour, I can almost see
him smiling, saying with cool, hard shiny dark eyes,
"Yeah you're bullshit, all right, a lot like your dad,
but in a different way, and if I had the chance and was
with you there tonight, I'd smack you in the side of your
head, with the back of my hand."

V.J.Q. 3rd 11/1/91

POEMS WRITTEN WHILE WAITING FOR A DAUGHTER

Twilight
and my fire is not under control.
Your mouth just might flare up under
certain circumstances:
Inspiration, provocation, rage, duress...
but who has the time or the spare kindling?

And as usual there is enough smoke to go around.

What her face recalls
are purely programmed impressions,
that upon reflection
dissolve in confusion and disaffection.

So I'm left to sharpen myself on you.
And I bet you
didn't feel a
thing.

Reluctant between the perfume and WD-40
useless her neck still turns stiff muttering idle ordinary
    discontent
like May as usual showing up persistently chilly and out of
    sorts.

All I have to do here is watch the light dwindle like ink flowing
all over the hours when your life hung in absence.

I am the man in your life before it began.
I will touch your head first.

So when you are at last born into that soft May night
at full moon around midnight cradle this moment
fashioned for you even before there was a you.

Breathe baby. Take that first inhalation.
Don't drown in the blood in the pull and push.
Be in my arms and bring some of that light
from heaven in your eyes.

We could use it here.

5/20/97

MAY 6, TUESDAY

Perfume alive in the lemons
sliced out into the air
sneaks around the bottle of beer
and gets into your jaw.
So night creeps or seeps,
maybe leaks out like the lid left off the Tupperware
Scent escapes somewhere wanted or else
that door opens on your selfish ass
what escapes?
All that can
with/without somewhere/someone to run to
under conditions of pressure
when the situation whips out of your control
and you are onboard for the ride.
So then ride it out
with periodic fits of piss poor prose.
Not like it wasn't in the odds.
Or even forever in the cards
52 for you or less; jokers are extra
Your choice of device
Smooth blank cubes
all dots removed.
So smother me in poison
and don't spare the carcinogens.

Still I wonder what's right at the end of your day
or left for that matter.
Did you have a report and "escalating situation"?

Ready to explode? To go.
Did you call for "back up"?

To reinforce this soap bubble of reality
where a pedestrian definition of "real" intrudes
and lances the veneer
And if you listen very carefully
"POP" goes the moment.

5/97

MAKING YOU

Your dad thought about making you
that June night lust passed into
dark morning when the moon did a chilly little
obscene jig and at last showed up
holding summer's hand.

And he was unsure
of everything
except the look in
your mother's eyes.

And the wind mixed it up
with the hissing, sighing small hours
creating your face
from their desire.

Each sound
resplendent
reverberation
warned him
to stop
but
that look in his eye
that look in her eye

got around to making you.

5/30/96

UNTITLED

It was a slow, rising, chilly, yellow moon
slicing crescent black paper cuts releasing
pinpoint jewels and there was just enough
shiver in them to go around

So you
contented yourself toying with the night
like it was a broken puzzle, inasmuch you gathered
from what he said all the pieces were indeed there,
but they all fit different pictures, at different times.

No wonder you're reluctant to tangle or tango with any
        of this
So you watch from a safe distance as he lights his
cigarettes like they were fuses.
And didn't you delight in the thought that you had
actually caught him in the act of trying to revive the
"I was the missing beat" routine, or was that "he thought he
was missing beat link", or maybe just a "missing link?"

But upon further consideration you discovered a way
to make all this so very dis-missable.

If the poetry stinks, you can always say, "I didn't see
what the big fucking deal was," or even if you were surprised
by how good it was, you could bail out with, " Well if it's
all such a big deal, why is he still hanging around here?"

But what you may never know
is how long it takes, or just what the walk is to find it.
Perhaps you're the one who's being sifted
always paring down to what won't fit through the
screen. The limited ears, the small eyes, a miniature world
of stilled perceptions.
Maybe that sky face puzzle is written in a language
you just don't speak or understand in the back street bar
in the middle of nowhere something
about this picture just blows
these words off the page. Maybe it's not about the page.
More about what escapes into thin air and
if you want it that's
where you'll find this, follow the sound, the eye, the heart
to a nameless place. You will recognize it
out of the corner of your eye.
And then it will wink at you.

10/97

YOUR SLOW GREEN SHEETS

(For J.)

I pulled and pushed the day away, then back towards me
Shook it minute by minute. Snapping at the hours like rubber
bands bound around the hands of the clock.

Such resistance.
The elements that comprised the steady march
toward your words. Always the expectation, wondering
        how they would match to my desire, my selfishness,
that busy menace of my day.

At every juncture, every opportunity the transitions tagged
and stuck. Having so little control over sequence,
duration or direction. The current just takes you.

It moves chilly May ever along, sagging, clogging, snagging,
snarling, pulling, sticking to the floor of the dull routine day
like the sole of your shoes adhering to the orchestra floor
of an old theater auditorium.

All I wanted was into the envelope to have at your words.
Dried past impressions hand motion
swept left across the face of the page.

And when at last I saw the green sheets spill your thoughts
all over my hands, only then did time flow even
still as my sigh stuttered in line after line.

Now in this notebook abreast the neck of the bottle
the head on the glass turns so slightly to light the spiral swirl
that binds these pages together.

Now it comes in close.
The confines of these blue lines stolen, swollen
as the sheet buckles with moisture that escaped my lips,
dropped onto the page and left something raised and bruised.
Not quite a kiss;
no, not an embrace of empty air.
Perhaps another grasp at an outline left
somewhere between vapor and vanishing.
But so damn close to all I have.
All I have. Of you.

5/97

THE BARNEY SONG

It was in a local sports bar that featured closed captioning
for hockey games on the four suspended tv's that night
right near the intersection where the "Beef an Carpet"
had a big flashing sign that blinked, "CAREFREE
HERCULON PORTERHOUSE WEAVES...BUY THE
FOOT OR POUND...DON'T YOU THINK YOU
DESERVE IT?" that I had been suckered into
reading some poetry one late fall night.

Wasn't it teeny tiny talent time at the open mike,
with the retarded shopping mall stand-up's telling
their miserable, desperate stupid jokes, the folk singers
twenty years too late, oozing sappy sincerity whimpering
songs that had been made into super market Muzak
already and then the MC gushed into the microphone,
"and NOW it's TIME for SOME POETRY."

I cringed.
Gathered up my papers and slouched up front.

I looked at the crowd, the sleepy, smug concentration
camp haircuts for the boys and girls, their features
carved out of ground beef and Maybelline and thought,
"Tonight may be the night they actually kill you."

However, out of the corner of my eye, I spotted this
one guy who had just walked into the bar. His dirty
beat work clothes, that tired face, the greasy cap,

the at large three day stubbled chin. Just your
standard exhausted working man, looking a little
pissed off and lot of drag ass. He plopped down on
the bar stool and his wallet, keys, cigarettes, lighter
all hit the bar at the same time. The bartender brought
him a beer immediately, wordlessly the guy lifted the
bottle and tilted back his head and drained off half
the contents.

The party crowd around him in Kathy-Lee Gifford
K-Mart dresses of pink and cream, the bleached teased
astronaut-wife's bouffant bubble-headed bimbos blathering
office gossip. The smoke rose around his head. He looked
service station black and white in their Technicolor
Penny's catalog world.
I thought, "Bingo".
If I can make this guy laugh, it all will be worth it.

So I launched into it.
Over the squealing and the high pitched sneering
I worked them over.
I read them the one about the son blowing his old man
away in the driveway at supper time with an AK-47.
Then a little number about masturbating with
Menthol Barbasol shaving cream.
Then another, and another, just spitting needles,
lancing those shampoo bubble veneers of reality.
One by one they shut up and stared open mouthed
at the microphone stand stunned.
The ending was especially brutal.
I crossed the line.
I dissed a local sports team.
They groaned, somebody muttered a muted threat.
And then it was all crickets,
Your basic conversation killer.

I looked at my tired man's shoulders for frame
of reference. He never did turn around.
But then his head dropped and started to shake
ever so slightly.

Picking my way throughout the snotty looks as I walked
back to my end of the bar to strangle my
pal who had gotten me into this, I noticed that the
guy's spot at the bar was vacant and the door behind
me had just swung shut and from the hallway came
within earshot, wave after wave of howling laughter.

Bartender comes over, shoots me a look like I've got
shit heels, and setting down a fresh beer says,
"This one's been bought for you, and by the way, do you
know what a lucky son of a bitch you are? Last week
I had some comedian knocked out cold up there."

I dead-panned him and said, "that's WHY I read POETRY."

Fall 95

REMEMBERING LUCY

That night Spring wasn't freshly exploded all over
the countryside. I ran across her as young colt in
another season. The path showed more Fall than anything
else. While the night whispered still a summer's gentle
pursed lip steam train of humidity.
Summer wanted to stay the night like a rapacious lover
who insisted upon clinging to your arm, grabbing for
too much nails in the crook of your arm, grabbing for
your hand pleading repeatedly, "I don't have to leave, do I?
............just please take me, just one more time."

Lucy with the long auburn mane.
Lucy laughing most of the time.
Except when her eyes drew silent because of hurt or a secret
pleasure you would never know the words to, but if you could
look back into her eyes as she desired, she would teach you
the tune.

But mostly you could just look and look all night
and never see the bottom.
The impossible long arms that bent and went around you
like the legs that went on forever.
And her middle held you in her handshake like a warm
friendly soapy washcloth.
When she broke into the weaving gait that slowly built
to a gallop all you could do was hold on and hope
to God she didn't decide to throw you.

Lucy, that night in that hot little room
when we touched off every combustible fiber there was
        to burn
in each other as we forced our bodies, alive with vigor
and youth into each other's pores.
You whispered at me from the fine sheen of
sweat that matted your hair and thick strands
pasted to your cheeks, your forehead, the sides of
your jaw line.

You took those arms and made this arc, a steeple that
pointed straight up and about my neck I can still feel
the moisture from your inner wrists upon my temples
dripping into my ears.
From the pale incandescent glow of your skin, while those
relentless orbs faded into passageways to other worlds

All steaming and burning with sensual delight,
from your mouth, from the full soft lips this spilled
out at me, "You drive me wild."

                                              7/95

HERE'S YOUR DUSTY TICKET

After a long drive.
Across the States
into a perfect June evening,
with selfish intent
to walk into a place
with cool red shadows
fans humming at work
You can rest your driving hands
ease off the pressing pedal foot.
Things in mind after the motion stops.
Heaven may not be like this,
however, this for the moment will do.

6/92

GARAGE NOTES

There once was a man who woke up one day and discovered that when he spoke he could only articulate himself by either cursing or quoting up-to-the-minute sport statistics.

"I AM so GODDAMN tired of this life of tedium and despair!"

And "Dante Bichette has 39 friggin home runs."

Summer 95

A COUPLE OF TIMES

Time to mow the lawn. Did he hate to mow the lawn?
He didn't think the lawn mowing part was so bad.
It was what he always had to think about while
doing it. The same sad shit, time after time. Was his life
developing into one long mercy fuck? Then he would think
about the guy who used to own this place. Word was that he
had dropped dead while mowing this yard. Every once in
awhile he would catch one of the neighbors sneaking peeks
in the slit of their drapes. Then he had to think about what
they were thinking about watching him mow the lawn.
The last thing he always had to think about was what was
that guy who used to do this same thing thinking
about when this was the last thing he ever thought about.
Like, how many good mows did he have left in him anyway?

Summer 96

AW PIN BALLS

Shake him a little, he'll tilt.

Summer 96

THE CHILDHOOD OF ERROL FLYNN

At eight years old in Australia Errol Flynn's father was a
scientist of Biology and did dreadful experiments on the
local animals like: the kangaroo rat or Zyurus, the opossums
or occasional Tasmanian Devil. Under his son's watchful
eye, he would split the subject open from stem to stern.

After much observation of his father's work,
young Errol fancied himself a scientist as well.
His field of research was focused in on the flock
of grey ducks that roamed in his back yard.

One afternoon he discovered they would eat just about
anything you threw at their heads.
His experiments showed that the ducks liked the hunks of
fatty salt pork from the cook's kitchen the best. Just
the smell of it in the yard drove them into a frenzy.
This fact was, however, not the most interesting observation,
the best part was that after fighting like hell for chunks
of the stinking mess, each duck would pass what he just
had eaten, in about a minute or two. You could time it.
It was fascinating.

It was nothing short of inspirational.

Errol's inspiration came in the form of getting about twenty
hunks of the fatty salt pork from the cook one afternoon.

Next stop was the supply shed for at least forty feet of nylon
   fishing line.

After some trial and error, some variations on a theme,
the correct formula for the right length of nylon wire,
exactly the precise spacing of the hunks of pork affixed
securely to said wire, was achieved.
Young Errol believed he had it all right.

He fed the lead chunk to the first duck. The duck swallowed
and passed the remains briskly. Errol then fed the next
duck in like a fresh piece on the same line. Sometimes the
duck was so worked up that he couldn't wait and greedily
gulped leftovers from the previous duck

Although it all sounds improbable and confusing to the
lay person, the experiment was a resounding success.
Soon there were somewhere in the neighborhood of a dozen
birds connected from beak to butt in a living quacking
duck bracelet. The bizarre configuration tugged and lurched
itself all about the back yard.

Such success led to ambition
Errol sold tickets to his friends in the neighborhood.
Word got around and they flocked in droves.

Near dinner time, Errol's father came home.
Professor Flynn witnessed his son's venture into
scientific inquiry and was horrified.

"Why you cruel little devil!" he gasped.
Then the elder Flynn broke his unopened umbrella
across his son's back.

Later in the evening, when pressed for an explanation of his
actions, young Errol explained he was only trying to be like
his father, the scientist.

Professor Flynn stared at his son, then had to turn away
very quickly.
And years later, Errol Flynn recalled that was
the only time he ever saw his old man cry.

Fall 92-94

WRITTEN ON THE LAST PAGE OF OCTOBER

Why would you ever hope that
they would come to the miniature low
rent tragic palace of your words?
How could you ever doubt your walk on
status upon the altar of the fun house?
And just who knows the sound that Mr. Simpleton Wind
makes when he does his "Howl" variations?
But after all, you should by now recognize
a theme to the tune of the sound that articulately eschewed
make on the way down or just simply over.
Which is better, because it's shorter.

So which way do your ears point tonight,
ever elusive audience?
I wish I knew what you were thinking.
I wish I even knew if we had enough in common
to fill a tea cup or fall down in the gutters at
an errant hour too drunk and laughing too hard to
get up, which of course made it funnier.
Or maybe you're just too cool to laugh.
Very educated, perhaps a literary connoisseur,
aw fuck, let's just shoot for full blown expert...
And there you are...
Right now somebody feels better
and of course
somebody else is getting a little pissed off.

All this might be pretty impressive if
for you there, sitting somewhere in the middle,
could suspend just enough belief to carry the rest of
our shattered ids that seem to find all this
....so stimulating.

So now it's "I've been in some big towns and
I've heard me some big talk, but when all that big
talk is through......"

You walk out into the great everybody lost night
that you face with only the static between your ears
either in a platoon or on solitary patrol.
Maybe we should put you out on point tonight.
And say, "Oh yes....please....stay in touch."
And do you?

Because it is when you feel you must
force just a little more
out of every night than they do,
you have to, don't you?

11/96

SATURDAY IN SCHENECTADY

Rained like hell
on a gray sad soiled worn out Broadway.
See we found this little place,
A corner bar called "Droids in the Mist"
and we went in and my brother-in-law ordered a round.

There was shuffleboard. An old table.
Twenty feet long at least
all pure honey hard wood veneer
salted lightly with canned sawdust.

There was this quartet of roofers from Philly
holding court.
Billy, Ed, Johnny and Murf.
Guess who was my favorite?

Too much rain. Drinking since noon.
Indoor stuff today waiting
for the weather to break
and finish the job, get paid and blow this cadaver
town.

"It's all in the weights," Murf spills out at last.
Blue flannel tucked in, pretty trim about fifty hard grey-top
about nine beers, four shots into it.
Not quite foreman material, however,

he would do as top dog for this crew.
His menacing demeanor gave you
a million reasons to stay alive
and alert, on line and carefully
on the listen.

Not to mention don't get mouthy.
He would shoot you this look every so often
like he was trying to make up his mind about you.
Deformed smart-ass or just another faggot?

Weights are what Murf really understands.
As in how much. What sort. Load factor.
He doesn't have to say it, but it's in his eyes
every time he looks at you and says,
"You're in over your head
with me there, sonny, so just play the game, real
polite like and don't even think of getting lippy
or I'll deck, drop and stack your ass. "
Good. Fast.
Nobody would see a thing.
After all, stupid mother-fucker was asking for it.

                                          Fall 92

FURTHER INSTRUCTIONS CONCERNING FRYING MAY

Would the steady chilly Saturday night May rain
put them all on edge?
Who would start begging first for someone
to talk with rather just listen to it rain May
and that sad jazz on the radio
even that runs out some chilly Saturday night.

May rained on all of them, didn't it?
From the start she couldn't, wouldn't get her story straight.
Sure she was through with Winter.
But she let him in to visit every few nights while
banging Summer on alternate odd days.
Her spring, you see, she felt was just never quite good
enough for anyone's season.

May arrived here
too hot too fast
packing mugginess damp sticky wet mohair sweater in
someone's embrace locked around your neck in
at midnight August in a small close room.

So I ask, "could we just once, have a little warm up at

first, rather than all this hot furious poking?"
And as usual I would leave before you come or
you would leave before I came
shallow as pavement mud puddle
and just about as steamy.

So in the dry heaves
came the loudmouthed thunderstorm.
All flashes of useless brilliance
All that loud talk, big bark.
But nothing really except a wave at time
most of it pure memory
it flashes just off the lakeside.

May fried something like a freshly shorted out
theater marquee with FURTHER INSTRUCTIONS spelled
out across its face and you know I think you
almost expected to be standing in a shower of cinematic sparks,
but all you really ever got was simply wet.

5/96

MAY 93

What time for this?
On April past too warm too fast
first fucking May all knuckles
no K-Y for you.
A Sneer for all seasons.
As everything else sneered back.
Or did the first thing vicious to anyone who came to
      mind first.

So it's just another spring poem;
there for you the unenlightened.
The educated consumer. The hanging Judge.
Each to his own
up to the neck
with a pure pink ass
you're soft
like a runny poached egg
just killing a little time wandering about
somewhere around the edge of toast
waiting for some repair crew to show up
and hook your snot back on line.

In the studied vernacular
of the age
when video is the papyrus.
With this hour's updated topical Minute;
or Pantheon to parody in factoid.

So no one refers to it as canned laughter anymore
as she drinks the ZIMA
lust's techno texture
while the fingers curl the grasp
about the new bottle for an old formula.

Once my side kick and I in a dirty beat up marshmallow
colored Granada that had rust scars like stretch marks
were stopped at the toll booths by a state trooper with
a stern, concerned face who wanted to know who the angel
faced gypsy raven was wedged between our suspicious
shoulders was?

"Oh, that's my girlfriend," I replied.

He looked doubtful.

I was sure he was going to say something about white
slavers, when instead he asked real business like,
"You got a registration here?"
I said, "Yeah what do you want first, the one for the car
or the girl?"

6/93

SKETCHES

Now you can't tell me
that anything is impossible while in this light.
It pours across the paper
I puncture it with my pen
and it just simply flows.

Like turning on the ear
and just receiving any available signals.
Go get the sponge of your id and wipe it all up.

You can see how connected I am
to the wolf tickets.
Completely committed to drawing his
face into the window.
So she pinned her hair up
and he got out his wallet
then her sweater hit the floor
While the boys in the sports bar
looked for the door.

But the light and sound poured
out of the air onto the page
the blotter of the pay phone ringing
like a page being turned.

1st Ave. And 84th
NYC Christmas 96

WELCOME TO NOREASTER SUNDAY AT SHEA STADIUM

Hung over, in the parking lot
striding smoking grey plume hateful of rain
so very damn happy
sick sad, but so much the stupid smile on his face.
Perched on a table overlooking the left field corner
high and dry watching the rain.
In the Mets beret, for chrissake.
Eating a barb-b-que pork sandwich
Ear stuck in the radio and the voices say,
"WE JUST HAVE WORD THAT..."
And down on the field the crew of umpires
come out from the runway behind home plate
and walk onto the sodden green diamond
and the crew chief
Harry Wendelstedt looks up at
the pouring sky and
"TODAY'S GAME HAS BEEN....."
He takes his arms and raises them
and makes the sign of the cross sideways.
Twice.
"......... CALLED OFF".

And don't he care less.
Walks over to the concessionaires
and tells them that
they can all go home
and have a nice Easter Sunday dinner
with their families.

And then he walks down the ramps
to outside the stadium where
now it is really pouring
upon the faces of those just arriving
and they don't know what he already knows.

He knows how to walk around in his dreams
or at the very least his poems.

April 96

WISH

Why do I see your face there.
That way,
with your expression set,
hanging open like a gate left ajar.

The eyes,
the way they look, the delicate features
defer, swing up.
The eyes that seem to hover the slight blink.

Was there ever that place
from where I sat on that evening
under the shadows from
the overhead lamps
I watch you listen
with your head on an angle.
I would make you laugh
with a smile so bright.
I feel you being drawn towards me.
You shoulders begin to arch
with your back to stretch into a "C"
and you feel yourself
sinking into my face.

Only words can frame that picture of us now.
Back in that place still swirling

like smoke in a mirror
as your hound's tooth skirt melts.

96

SUMMER

The heart beat night
sounds as a knock upon the door
in the dream where I'm pacing from corner
to window from pillar to post
unable to reach the knob.

I know that the street sings
while hissing insinuating rain
washes all the color into torrents
of blues yellow bumpers
leaving red eyes
while the rain colors the street
It's bathed in chilly light
cool blue and standing red
glare at each other and taunt
"What's matter, nothing 'Arty' to say about orange?"

94

YOUR LAST LETTER

Your last pages dove-tailed
completely into the chaos of my desk top
the words you had written kept flirting
with a box of Rosebud match sticks by
whispering, "come on just one of you just once
come out and strike attitudes with me, we could
start a fire that might put this guy out of his
misery once and for all."

96

TUESDAY NIGHT LESSON PLAN AT THE LITTLE HOUSE

Tonight the guards brought Raffy in the classroom
with the side of his face blooming in fresh strawberries,
one eye so bloodshot it looked like a city street map
of Scranton. He smiled at me as he sat down to his workbook
and when I didn't ask (I never ask) Raffy simply stated,
"little disagreement up on F block."
Giving him a pencil I wondered out loud if he would be
O.K. to read
Raffy looks back at me and smiles from his freshly
detonated face and says, "Hey, I've got two eyes."

6/96

UNTITLED

And there she was again.
He still had the same thoughts.
This fantasy centered around a harness.
You could suspend the contraption from a door jamb
or eye hook screwed into a support beam in the ceiling.
Hopefully the harness would not be a complicated affair.
Attention to detail was essential. Items like rabbit fur
strips to prevent chafing were a nice touch.

She would have to be placed hanging straps by her torso
with the legs placed through the loops so that her feet
were about eight inches off the floor.
Now I see an alabaster oyster gingham
dress with pale blue lace.
One of those old fashion Italian tee shirts underneath.
You could restrain her hands at the wrists. (At first)
There should be a lot of bounce and play in the action
of the harness swing.

You could approach her from a number of angles.
There could be a good deal of discussion about that.
Coming up under the dress from below could be a solid start.
Most of all.....It would take time.... perhaps a lot of time.
Panties on....panties off. Merely a matter of preference
Sliding them down with the tongue and gently tugging with
the lips and teeth seems likely.

The pivotal action of the swing in the harness would be key
as would be patience.

You could enter her standing on a kitchen chair or step-stool.
From the rear first. Then face to face, with her long legs
wrapped around your hips. Careful. Remember she's the one
that's safely secured. And they have been known to buck
when they really get into it.

Just try and keep this thought in mind.
Do this correctly and you'll get to her
like open flame takes wax off fabric.

11/96

SATURDAY AFTERNOON
IN THE CAN

After I make out the class request sheet,
After I check the Alpha list in the booking room
for the block number on my incoming charges.
They move them around from cell to cell,
more than you might think, the usual squabbles,
Just can't seem to get along with the neighbors.
Just can't seem to crap on the open bowl, not really
in the center of the room, but partitions never were
part of the floor plan, so it would make you take less
on your tray and probably seldom ask for seconds of
the brown stuff.

The C.O.'s bringing them down the hallway.
They walk inmates, but sit down students,
so quickly and almost always get down to work
pretty fast. Their books, papers and pencils
all laid out for them, it all happens pretty fast
they always seem to want to get into it, to maybe
escape for an hour, like if only they could get back
to being in school and maybe that time before when
everything was all right.

A second chance to escape all the trouble.

I walk about the tables to answer any questions.
After that I turn up the small black radio in the corner
of the room up ever so slightly so that we all can hear
the Benedictine Monks singing Gregorian Chant
"Christus Factus est pro Nobis".

4/96

WE WILL BE RUNNING OUT OF NUMBERS SOON

I could be the Jack Kevorkian of poetry.
You might call me when your poems
are sick, looking terminal and there's
just no hope and I will assist you
putting them all to sleep, maybe dream
and wake later, feeling better.

Or I might be just writing Value Jet Poetry.
This vehicle will either take you on your
desired destination cheaply or will engulf
 you in a fireball that will dump you a
char cinder into a bottomless swamp in Florida.

Oh.............so you've already been there.
Now I'm not sure whether to remit or recant.

Because the toothpick is in my pocket
and there sit the boys in the can.
And the boys guarding the boys in the can.
They hope for parole
I hope for a toothpick
in my pocket.

Your letter on my hat.
A picture of an ocean beach, dunes
where I would like to be with you.

The girl that sits home.
Wondering about his moods.
Wondering if she's pregnant

The money in my pocket
burning a hole, burning a hole
to match the ditch out in the street.
A deeper edition of gutter to skip.

But all day the time passing, passing running out.

The ashes on the bar.
The list of things to do with you.

9/96

THE DYBBUK DREAMS

It was in the first few nights of the New Year
when all promise and disaster were as unopened mail
that the past had a walk in his sleep.

The Dybbuk's hands opened old drawers
shuffled through forgotten pages
Pausing to repeat a line of a letter
here and there.

Ashes were stirred and long dormant old flames set free
to flicker. Then the night faces could dance once more.
Night faces coming back to visit shining
eyes to glow back into.

Another year rolling itself out like an immense black wing .
Your sleeping form swept along in this night flight,
those waking hours, now the specter, this was the soul
strolling hand in hand with the eternal freedom of
time asleep.

She walked once more upon the moors, in a chilly thick fog.
Here where she had always known that he waited for her
In between anger and consequences,
in this dream scape of quicksand recall where mushroomed
marsh islands of what might have been.

They both returned to this shadow realm of still photographs
hung and propped in the endless stark arms of winter.

Here where the past stood naked and true.
Both came with small hands grasping deep into the heart's
pocket. Each visited at different points
along the dream curve, with separate dependencies and
versions of the same story.

They left messages here for each other.
The last word over and over. The promises of reconciliation
and forgiveness. The sensation they shared of never being
able to meet face to face again, outside of this place
of half light sand deep grey pools. Always to return to
the same beaten path, in the corner of the dream.
This place where the images of each other's faces
in those frozen photos snared arrested looks
and eyes of love and delight that once were shared.

They both returned to this place, every so often
to get a face full and
look down at the other's footprints
left in the path
from the night before.

95

MAUL SET

Kaufman's parking lot sits
with the outlines fading twilight
half empty or half full
according to your consumer confidence.

Replicant industrial grid spread out in hologram
3-D horror. The blue bright print aglow electricity
in knots.
A view to marvel indeed.
Brilliant brutal and impossible to live in.
Except as a puck in the crowd
Inside this virtual reality Nintendo smegma.
Here's to tonight at the games with full soundtrack
and prestigious commercials
while we at home all wait for a regional break
to give benediction in I told you so's
to John Dos Passos
who wrote the original formula
as did ever Henry Miller do the script treatment
about the war to end all wars being over.
But the future just ran out of juice
and all the small engines had bad hair days.

Just as last of the roast beef sunset slices the
access ramps into black spaghetti, one of the civilian units
is intercepted by the patrols signaling compliance with a
triple set of pustule bubbles of red, white and blue strobe
beams that cast ghastly shadows in a wide circle.

There is the dull metal snapping of automatic
weapons fire briefly until there is a sucking sound
and a flash of brilliance, followed by the concussion
of the car's gas tank exploding.

Patrol Alpo six tango Romeo and Map reference: Arbry's
Grid Map 4EY MARK 23:57 hrs. has just scored a bulls eye;
short range missile back talk deterrent system.
Log book shows probable cause.
Strictly routine.

Sheraton Inn
5/93

THE MAP ON THE DESK

I ran my finger across the red and black lines
that were going somewhere and struggled to recall
an odd poem I once sent you from Pittsburgh one fall.
I lived on the map in those days.
I tried very hard to force those red and black lines
into my blood. It was my belief that motion would
at least provide a moving target for the blues.
It didn't work.
A limping, stuttering, nastiness
adhered itself to my shadow.
After a time, I began to wonder
why I was always embracing that
black bucket pouring
out anothers' bitterness,
hatred or confusion.
I was always getting soaked.

I covered the desk with a book of maps
and I looked at the names and I said them out
loud till the sound of my own voice was a stranger
in my ear.
Looking for consolation I began digging through the
metal draws below pawing clutter and counted on holding
onto the nothing, if I could find it.

Oh, there was the holding on.
Nothing noble.
More like noble nothing.
Always the holding on.
Why do the cowards always
seem to talk the loudest?
The conversations loaded
with beery inquiries with
the information operators
who showed more concern
than you did looking for
that forgotten area code.

You could walk down that street
and glance in a store front to catch
the pontificating phantom
in the plate glass shrugging.
I live on the other side of the tracks now
just a couple of blocks down the street from our old apartment.

You were right after all.
He was just another man
with a hole in his face.
Sure. The big Crimson period.

But when I think of you now
placed in the middle of this production number
a lot of it comes back intact, shipping tags and all.
Sits right there. Still. Waiting up to be moved.

Everything else may drift a bit.
But you just never seem to quit
or guess just what it is
you still seem to have got coming.
I could rent you the original shackles.

I've kept a spare set in a box
back in the bottom of the closet.

I never got the original set off.

Did you know you're still circling Second Street.
Looking for Antelope at four in the morning
that night you couldn't remember
which dead end was mine.

And you didn't find me
asleep with another.
Just the blue Rambler
asleep in the driveway.
And you couldn't remember walking in the street light's
veil from the room to room
to find me
crying the hardest tears
I ever knew at sunrise
on my knees next to the bed.

10/9/94

TUESDAY AND THURSDAY EVENINGS

On Tuesday
the tall girl with brown swinging mane
runs up the alley barely contained in a brief tunic
made of sunset and bent aluminum side apartment doors.
Her legs pump the loose gravel.
She stops to consider
the rented yellow truck whipping around the corner, leaning
to one side with an unbalanced freight, following poorly
written directions to a disputed destination.

Driver's attention is arrested by the tall girl's gait.
Distracted, he almost runs the stop sign.
There's a piercing shriek as the truck's tires clutch
at the asphalt's face.

Driver sighs at the empty alley.
Thinks he may be lucky
but isn't sure about what.
On Thursday
slide those shadows over here
across the page where I can misinterpret them better
My studied art of getting the story wrong.
Withhold my complicity, the third degree conspiracy
like a drunken court stenographer
who records in archaic short
hands notes that will be undecipherable after he's dead.

Then the predicable mistrial, the sustained perpetual confusion
like a hung jury's deliberations.
On Tuesday
At this time of the evening the bar has a hard bright glare
from the street that makes the inside of this place and
everyone look worn, old and beaten. My face smeared
a dozen colors smolders. None of the light at this
time of evening warms anything. Sharp sullen edges abound.
So we drain that bitter cold liquid from bottle
to fade that light, round the harsh menacing edges
the day cut in our faces. Knowing in here it's just a matter
of time till all the cacophony fades.
Motion then rides time in a black harness. Your flesh
completing another lap towards finish line death with a
clipboard and pencil to sign you in. Record your time
demanding you surrender your life. Pay attention forever
to the everything that forgets you ever existed.
On Tuesday
Last night I had a series of dreams. The most vivid image
was that I was swimming in the Sound during sunset. The
water was a smooth, slow, rippling blue blanket.
She was gently floating naked on her stomach
Her shining skin a melted mirror translucent
in liquid reflection setting golden flesh afloat.
The sky all over her.
I drifted by lost in the tide.

On Thursday
What is the correct shade of your face
at that certain hour in a twisted twilight guess.
I recalled you on that Saturday night before the
world faded you.
When you walked in the door and placed the palms of your
hands upon my shoulder blades.

I always know when it's you.
I dream about when I actually can turn around
and have you face to face there.

You, that full dish of lime sherbet.
So very, very cool hair pulled, piled up in a bun
above the clammy sticky stupid bar
Your eyes shining for me, smiling lime lines
on that sherbet dress.

At last I turned around already knowing what
I'm going to think,
What a dish, what a dish, what a dish.

On Thursday
Could we get this straight once
the faces, time and intent
while June impossible
in his face taut and strong with loss.
Those beads of sweat loss grief strewn
pearls pushed out clear under duress
of the moment.

The telling in between
when that luxury has all but run out.
Then June silent still
stalks alive outside your grasp pretty sticky

in that hot bar room sagging or was that singing
pushing a kid's plastic lawn mower;

"I can't hear you"
"I can't hear you"

On Tuesday

And all that hard talk
suddenly went fiction or just plain weak
in light of revision
such neglected sunshine
squandered daily
in routine via black top
singing while we can
let me out....
You ignored me all day....
And now you want my attention?

So you're left to argue
between too wide and too bright
and see what you come up with;
15 pounds of enough
in a 10 pound bag.

On Thursday

Clear evening singing
in a tuneless prolonged sigh
with a limited attention span
despite yourself interested
for a moment between consecutive mirrors
your voice found that familiar ear
given in trust and perhaps
for a moment in a fashion
that abounded in a forgotten world
before contrived
visual images saturated
all perception and displaced
original sin to the sack and
ash cloth of independent thought.

Sing me my hoax as blessed derivative systems
beyond the fingers suspended at loose ends.

While for you there is so much

of so little
in all this.

So go then you gentle idiot
fill that air or page
with your images of small cheap
pictures to explain.
While August growing late
will shake something loose.
A certain tightening
in public is called for.
(But time does not permit)
And as for keeping your distance,
(I should say not).
And until your heart's content?
(Sure. If we can find it).

Summer 1997

HIS MTV LOVER

She was a Fiona Apple look alike
from Teaneck subletting a loft in Tribeca.

She was either gonna be a model or work in advertising.
Her boyfriend had a goatee and wore cut off shorts in
winter.

At first they had a lot in common.
They both liked Pearl Jam.
Hated Rap or Metal and ate at the salad bar
at Ponderosa every Tuesday and Thursday.
Terrified at the prospect of AIDS or getting pregnant
she would neck with him maybe an occasional hand job;
but since that one time after one too many Bailley's
the rubber had broken in the middle of it and she said,
"She wasn't gonna do that with him anymore".

Sometimes he slept over on the couch.
In the middle of the night, he would wake up and creep
up the ladder to watch her sleep.

He wondered if she dreamed or what.
One time he watched her play with herself in her sleep.
He looked at the long thin form under the white sheets
and wished he could crawl under there with her...

Later that Fall her father reeled her back in with
his check book and he came back to the loft and a couple
of Thrill Kill Kult freaks answered the door and said they
didn't know her or where she was.

He never saw her again.

Years later she wakes up in the middle of the night.
She gets up out of her bed to look out the windows into
the empty silent streets of Nanuet unable to get back
to sleep. She tries to fight off a memory of him. Then
succumbing to it, she is surprised to discover she can't
recall the features of his face clearly. She sits down on
the end of the bed to smoke a Marlboro Light. It makes her
dizzy. The exhaled smoke hangs in the heavy stale haze about
her head. She starts to cry and thinks, "I'm never going
to be a model".

She crushes out the cigarette and puts her head back
down on the pillow. Her new spiked hair cut feels odd
on the sheets. The dried tears make her cheeks itch. As she
stretches her legs, she scratches her nose. On her fingers
she can smell herself as she drops off into a dream.

She dreams of someone in the far corner watching her
sleep.

95

END OF OCTOBER

The day had been the kind of grey
that elected itself spokesman
for the afternoon.
The voice chilled with a certain
knowledge of pale blue diluted
into a chilly white that promised lassitude.
The voice is saying the seasons
are in collision and we are in the locking in.

Fall has spent weeks gathering on the ground
and Winter as of yet is disinterested
in the whole business
refuses to go to work
so the ground shuffles the leaves like
a card shark ready to
deal ice cube deuces for your hand.

The time of the mask comes and goes.
So the night fills and drains costumes.
Stalking Quick Bank; Celebrity hero murderers,
Syntax gender victims seeking damages; Purple
suited stunt persons' blubbering compassion and
politeness; decapitated rock stars, mutilated
millionaire ex-cheerleaders and just plain folks
caught in the crossfire, car jacking drive-by
random acts of brutal insanity of choice or chance.
Legions of green, yellow, red, black and white
three foot high grunting kicking punching power

midgets morphing into respected connected influential
public officials and politicians that are shaping the
course of personal liberty in your lives.

The traditional allotment of vampires, ghouls, demons
and blood thirsty fetus snatching liberal aliens.
What freedom the night affords.
All the secretaries become waitresses, the waitresses
become actresses, the actresses become whores, the whores
become Raggedy Ann's become princesses, who become
gypsies and then as the dawn breaks they all turn back to
secretaries.

The great hangover of our self-deception on
all souls night.

I watched you swim the twilight
while the trees are stripped of their delicate garments.
You are swallowing the dusk in buckets
drowning in a swirl of mad flight as the undertow of
the wind sucks and pushes brittle leaves dragging
their finger nails along the sidewalk.

On the way home, I'll buy you a pumpkin
and we can carve a face into it and take turns
guessing whose it is.

92

RUMPUS ROOM

Good light fills the room
of past come now to see the future
here in this blond snotty pine
that hugs the shoulders down to
the red soul tiled rumpus room.

Your neck gets the hook on the back of the closet door.
All of them, hanging here,
as if it had been, just a matter of spare ties
and being given just enough throats.

Back here is where has-been hurricanes blow to
after they have left forever the sea.
Names are checked in at the door.
Past posted mail forwarded or not
finds its way here by the hand of diminished winds.

And aren't we always waiting for just one blow more?
Either by wire or chance or door;
Send in my favorite colors;
let even the diminished winds, have one more roar;
all that you get back here is, "How are ya?",
"Where ya been?", "Are you really still sore?"
All my favorite colors ... sent back here
either by wire or chance or door;
Aren't we always awaiting for just one more?

They come in, head shaking from side to side;
saying "How did we ever get here from there?"
"You should have seen me that night, I stopped the room
cold, backed them all up with free shots and beer.
I got mentioned in the hourly CNN updates,
they all said, this was supposed to be my year."

Now you'll find me here in another rumpus room,
And I don't feel like a "has-been" hurricane
It's not the gale I find I need
Just a way to blow off shore
a sail to fill, a face to light;
It's not the gale I find
I lack;
We just need a sharp smooth tack
into another's coastline.

And aren't we always waiting for just one more?
either by wire or chance or door;
All my favorite colors
at the hands of diminished winds.
It's "How are ya? Where were ya? Are you STILL SORE?"

Maybe this is your year..for just one more roar.

11/89

CASHING-IN

America with the crazy Aunt in the forbidden closet.
Her name, a lie that would never be faced
here in the what's left over from the last frontier
left on earth.

Our rich heritage.
Spread the disease;
destroy the existing culture.
kill the locals,
replace with criminals
imported slaves in cargo holds.
Put the religious fanatics in charge.
Set up with witch trials,
publicly humiliate and invalidate
anyone suspected of any individuality.
Denounce the mother country. Refer to ask the old whore.

More persecutions.
Kill the locals.
They're so..so.. Ordinary.
Gonna need more slaves.
A whole lotta slaves.
Fight a war over ownership.
A bloody regional dispute
fought with primitive weapons.
Butcher tens of thousands.
Great news.
You win.

Free the slaves by redefining ownership
transfer their title to the budding corporation
by transferring power from the many to the few.
Water that little corporation.
Re-name her baby America.
Kill more locals in her honor.
For her birthday break the unions
What a gift idea for the coming of age.
Dabble in World War.
Let it fuel industry.
Have the carnage make a select few citizens wildly
rich.
As powerful as Gods.
Let the general population grow fat and lazy
while the majority have their dignity and means of

making a living devastated daily.

Propagate and glamorize the illusion machines
Let Madison Ave. redefine dreams.
Let product ownership replace identity.
Have Media stars transcend one's personality.
Take those dreams and put a big price tag
on them.
Keep it out of reach. Put promise.

Promise those dreams.
Rich ones. Cheap ones. Have a sale.
Bargains. Bargains. Bargains.
Stock um out at Wal-Mart.
Burn them all down.
Have a fire sale.
Sue the fire department.
Collect the insurance in the meantime.

Invest the surplus cash
in fossil fuel wars and
re-education programs
for those pesky poor.
Fortify the power citadels,
Kill the locals.
Have another revival.
Let the cities burn, then rot from the inside.
Year two thousand's right around the corner.
Start talking judgement.
Let the religious right in the jury box.
Let them redefine all laws.
Perhaps inquisitions at half time at the
Superbowl.
Nice touch.
Hold action on the side bets
Who's gonna come first the Bills or
the second coming.

America with the crazy Aunt's skeleton in the closet
pure white bones
no flesh, no stink
lifeless, pure, sterile.
In terminal denial
about the lie that will never be faced.
What we did to the last frontier on earth.

We cashed it in.

Now what about the ocean floor?

7/93

FLUBBER GAS AND THE END OF THE WORD

I dreamed one night that time stopped in black and white
in 1963 on the Disney lot.
During the court room scene Fred McMurray gave a speech
about every day being ground hog day in America these days.
Then Ed Wynn turned into the Secretary of Defense.
Ordered in the swollen vegetables to present as evidence.
Slowly the air raid sirens began to wail outside
the windows.
All the journey men character actors turned to look
at each other. The old one that had a head like an
80 year old tortoise in the role as the bailiff
stuttered out something that sounded like, "..but...but.
This isn't in the script".

The realization dawned on them
that all this was
was the high point in their career.

The first shock wave pushed all matter in contact blur
then sucked the matter back in reverse elastic.
Those who could still think
experienced the sensation
(Or was It the sensation had him?)
Their lungs were coming up the throat.
(One at a time)
Next, of course, the predictable fire ball.

After it all cooled
the Son of Flubber came back
and after surveying the blackened moonscape
with the atmosphere
freshly ripped off its hinges
and demanding an accounting,
The Son of Flubber snarled,

"Just who in hell is responsible here?!"

The size of the nothing that responded
was astounding.
No wind.
No light.
No air.
Christ. The nothing startled him.
"Oh yeah", he went, "I forgot."

Winter 95

ROAD KILL

His story didn't make any sense.
No one bought the details about the cruise control
just sticking open, that's what he said at first,
then he changed his story to..."I was just reaching
over for the thermos of coffee on the floor on the passenger
side...", on and on it went.
What was closer to the truth is that he just dozed off at
the wheel. Went to sleep to dream. Dreaming at sixty-five on
the black to dual lanes, dreaming about going that fast and
being at the wheel like some
hideous recurring nightmare about
having to hold a direction, but not being able to see clearly
out of the windshield. Dreaming about his obscene little
rent-me video life back in Wisconsin.
Dreaming how, one day he would quit
this damn driving all night and work in his
brother's underwriting office. Dreaming about that waitress
in Denny's in Pennsylvania, who wouldn't fuck him and
thought him a queer little rat runt and she didn't give a
good shit if he drove a truck or turned insurance junkie.
So the wheels drift.
Load of Anderson's got shift
twenty five gross
storm windows blew up broke
and wished to God he was in a little row boat.
It took the force and concussion of the impact
to wake him up.
He was very much still in the process of laying her

down on the midnight blacktop in a shit storm
of orange sparks and asphalt with steel ripping like
steak knife necking with aluminum foil.
Forty thousand dollars of freight run into seventy dollar an
hour drainage ditch, bent the frame like a Mueller's egg
noodle. Everything in his box did a Dorothy and he was the
strawman and was going to have to pay attention to the man
behind the curtain.

He walked away from it.
He felt so guilty over his lack of injury,
he had his arm put up in a sling.
Next morning he showed up with an old Instamatic;
to take some pictures for his brother.

MEMORY KIT

(For D.B.)

Wake up.
Don't speak.
Remember if you dreamed.
Don't worry... you did.

This morning you have the time to recall.
The dreams.
Don't be concerned if you only have a glimmer.
Not a story.
A fragment will work.
A look. Color or word.
Walk outside.
Smell the air.
What comes back?
Test patterns your eyes.
See the outlines of
the years past in yard.
Coffee?
Sure, why not.
While making it
listen for the voices
in the kitchen.
Any echoes?
Walk back outside with the coffee.

Now look around again.
Take what you're thinking
and speak it out loud.
Do you have your instrument?
Go back in the house and get it.
Strum.
No don't concentrate
on anything.
Just let the past wash into the now.
There is something there.
Grab it and pull into the present.
Let it breathe.
Breathe life into it.

Start the machine.
Then ignore it.
Let it record
your thoughts
the reflections

the chords.

Remember to the paper or the tape.
To the air, the woods, the mountains.
Do anything you need to do
to get at the thing.
But
don't delay.

7/96

GROWING RESPECT

You know there's a growing respect in this country
for commercials that look a lot like this one.
Compelling emotional knee jerk images
that invoke quick calculated gut reactions.
Fuzzy soft re-enactments
of disjointed sentiments and nostalgia with
babies, puppies and toddlers on the porches of big wide
safe affluent houses with big yards and Grand Pa.

There's a growing respect in our country these days for
images with the voice on the sound track curdling
just like this one. Pouring on the guilt inducing
micro-message about responsibility jingoism and the common
sense in Orwellian right thinking.
The self-assured tones that want to seduce you to take none
of this manipulation in separate components.
Just accept and swallow the whole superficial
cable contrived reality play at face value.

You know there's a growing respect in this country
for letting commercials like this do your thinking for
you. Just sit there and react to our presentation of your
point of view.

After all we are the professionals
We selected this music to use as the soundtrack.
It invokes clear simple notes of all-knowing
simplistic drivel. Can't you feel your eyes water

to those slow, soft cascading C chords as the last
suggestion is superimposed over a little blonde
dolly hugging the pink plastic baby:

Latitude: What a beautiful privilege.

5/93

IDEA FOR AN USHER

Between one and four
An abrupt voice blurted from the scanner:
"Move in the derricks."
Fearing exposure he tore apart what was left standing first,
till the dumpster out front was half full
with remains of a small town tornado;
and a mild pallor of October's night,
the kind that hiss warm stray cricket sinuous
exhaled on the back of your neck.

If you were outside (that is).
Instead the reclining form on the bed
in sleepless window face full of a small black and white
leaking grey out of a tv screen.
The sheets look like waves frozen mid-curl.
Along a coastline of quilted
entanglement with discontentment.

Everyone that night it seemed to him were, to varying
degrees, prisoners of bad scripts, poor lighting and vulgar
choreography direct from Devil's Island to The Hanoi Hilton.

Meanwhile you don't dare look out of the corner of your eye
toward the direction of the bedroom curtains hung in a slit,
In which a bone faced moon sickle sliced and
crawled left to right.

He must have nodded off
for a few minutes as the brittle delirium
mumbled in the night speak's vernacular
which at last got a word in edgewise
saying, "Here slip this penny under your wrist watch."
And repeat after me.
If should you glimpse of me this nightmare lone
and recall in kind the light on the fade
where strange outlines dance in the bedroom wall half made
those stark traces suggest certain faces.
Just be sure you call their names first.

You've always wanted an owner's manual for all this.
Just one clear illustration of the location and operation
of the panic bars on the exit doors toward dawn.
Then you might at last shove once and for all
in a sleepwalking terror the right piece of metal
to obtain release.

92

HER MTV LOVER

A couple of weeks after the semester ended and
Ray Rad had moved back home to his folks' house in
a suburb near Albany, over a bowl of Just Right one
morning his father had looked at Ray's newly pierced
left nostril and had snarled. "O.K. Goddamit, that's
enough!" Ray looked surprised. I mean what was this
guy's problem, he thought I'm up at the crack of dawn
(it was 9:30) and I'm having breakfast with this pain in the ass
and all he wants to do is break my balls.

Ray's ears were still ringing from band practice the
night before. Ray's band "The Singing Sperm Smelts" had
a big gig coming up at the local dump next week. I mean
didn't this old asshole know the pressure he was under?

The elder Rad looked at his son's shaved head and wanna
be beard and salvation army oversized clothes that stank of
stale smoke and beer and shook his head.

"O.K. Ray, now you have your nose with an earring too,
that makes the pierce count at five. What's next your
fuckin' tongue?" Ray laughed. "Don't be crazy dad, how
could I sing with that? And besides, the bass player already
had that done two weeks ago."

Ray's dad slammed down the morning paper knocking over
his coffee cup. "Listen, you look like a holocaust victim

from a fashion concentration camp. I want you to cut the
crap and start looking for a job for the summer."
"But dad, what about the band?"
"Forget the band you idiot, I want you to start looking
today, I hear that the Burger King is hiring. Now take the
friggin jewelry outta your face, shave off the filthy fuzz
and get your ass in some human clothes and by the time I
get home tonight, you had better be working somewhere.
Period."

After Ray's dad had left for work, Ray Rad went back
upstairs and jumped into bed. Around two in the afternoon,
Ray called Arfy the bass player with the pierced tongue
for the "Singing Sperm Smelts" and invited him over

They sat up in Ray's room watching MTV passing the joint

back and forth discussing their song list. "Well, I think we
ought to open up with "The fish has no balls." Arfy shook his
head and lisped over the pearl tear drop earring in his tongue,
"Nopeth I thinketh we had better starth with 'Nazi Angel
stompth.'" Just then a report came on the MTV that a
popular young band leader had blown his head off.
"Whoa!" said Ray.
"Wowth." said Arfy.

Later that night Ray's dad parked his Mini-Van in the
driveway and as he got out was hit with a burst of
automatic weapon fire. He was dead before he hit the ground.
From up in his bedroom window
Ray was a bit surprised how fast the barrel
of the AK-47 had gotten hot. As the grey
heavy smoke hung about the room, Ray looked down at his

old man blood splattered, twitching in the driveway. And
he said softly to himself, "Would you like that for here
or to go?"

94

IN OCTOBER WHEN THE PRICE WAS RIGHT

Outside that night sounded like
they were moving the whole damn thing
by engaging deep gears to grind.
While gyrating iron teeth to filings
drained lubricants dry for thick couplings
deliberately pulling something apart in the darkness.

There is the smell of diesel fuel everywhere.
It almost works.
Now if there's no sparks......we're in business.

The faces watching, glow vacantly, flushed with excitement
of actually being in the studio audience.
The camera pans slowly the entire length of the risers.
Squeals of gaiety as a wireless microphone is passed
around and everyone got a chance to identify themselves,
where they were born and one special shallow wish.

When the red light clicks off.
The stage hands reappeared with the bull whips
and the host pulled back a lever and that sound
and that smell filled the room once more.

If it hadn't been for that short in the applause sign...
The price would still be right.

10/92

ALL OUTTA ORANGE

(For F. O'H.)

I walk into the corner bar. Young artists are hanging their
work on the walls. The appear quite serious and sullen.
The dinner crowd strolls in. Ignores the paintings.
I have a look around at the art. Some styles appeal to me
more than others, however, I like the whole idea of it
just fine. After awhile the artists get up at the podium
down the far end of the bar to make a statement about their
work. Dinner crowd buzzes with small talk. Ignores the
Artists. Artists respond by cutting their mumbling short and
retreat to an especially dark corner in the back.

It's business as usual. Bartender comes over bringing me
a fresh bottle of beer. I say, "I need you to do me a favor,
it's opening day, could you put the baseball game on the
television." She shrieks, "I hate you. " My eyebrows flip
up. This is serious. I've devoted the better part of a
lifetime living by a simple, moral code: "Never piss your
bartender off." I scramble for an apology. She meanwhile
is dutifully changing the channel while whining, "but
there's a HOCKEY game ON." I recover. "Not to worry,
change it back I only had a cursory interest in it anyway."
She looks at me as her face twists into a question knot and
says, "A WHAT INTEREST???"

I give up. An "orange" interest, I riff out loud.

She shrugs. Tends to other customers. I scribble in my note book;

"When Poets speak in color they are stuck with ears.
When the Artist paints with pigment the picture is at the
mercy of the eyes. So it stands to reason that the latter
is an image with no sound and the former is all hearsay.
The punch line is, however, you can't dream of deaf
awake anymore than you can ignore the blind into seeing.

The bar starts to fill up. A quartet of beautiful
women arrives. Sauntering studs strike attitudes
accordingly. Dinner crowd ignores them. Young poet takes
the position at the podium. Tries to work his stuff out.
Dinner crowd manages some variation on a theme. One of
them makes a snotty aside. Poet cuts it short. Smattering
of indifferent applause percolates like stale popcorn
smothered in excess vegetable oil.

Man next to me in backwards ball cap and earring smirks,
"Enough of that sorry ass shit,"scans the hockey game and asks
"so what's the score?"

A twilight tide leaks into the bar room, its last gasp coats
customers, artists, poets with a radiant fragile vermillion
shroud and for a shimmering instant a brilliant painting is
born, gasps and dies. Dinner crowd ignores it.

Bartender comes back with a cold one on the house.
I sigh relieved. All's well. We're pals again.
Host of the evening lurches up dejected. The night that
showed such promise is deflating rapidly. I try and help
by saying, "You know this reminds me of last night. I woke
up at three in the morning and couldn't get back to sleep.
I'm worrying. My wife has the baby in less than a month.
Not only is our house a little brown shoe box that needs

a new roof for a couple of grand, it's way too goddamn
small. I'm worrying that the new kid's bassinette will have
to go on top of the television. I'm worrying that any day
now an inter-galactic kidney stone asteroid will make mince-meat
of this teetering global psychoses and some anchor person
on CNN will shit their pants on air, live in front of
40 million viewers. And then what? A nuclear free
winter for the next four years. Might be a little rough
ordering a pizza. So I'm worrying more. What if I lose my job
teaching in the jail? Worse yet, what if I keep my job
teaching in the jail? I'm worrying. I've still got
many bad habits. I drink too much. I smoke too much.
I'm never gonna pass muster at the social behavior
inquisitions of the new witch trials of the year 2000.
And to top it off, friggin Bob Apodaca is the friggin
N.Y. Mets pitching coach.

So I get up and go into the living room and turn on
the TV. I find Federico Fellini's Satyricon blazing away
life with the characters speaking in cryptic poetic verse.
As usual every other scene there is this set of eyes staring
out at you, watching you as you watch the scene. It took me
away. I forgot my troubles as I immersed myself in the story
of two young men having an epic adventure in grotesque Rome
as it shattered and collapsed under the sheer weight of
perversion, ignorance and brutality. It was great, ever
see it?
I looked up. I was getting the hairy eyeball all
around. The woman sitting next to me was looking at me like
I was an escapee from Heaven's Gate and was fixing to order
a round of phenobarbital and vodkas.
The bartender was polishing the glasses
shaking her head, she had heard this all before; nobody
within earshot had the foggiest notion of what the hell
I was talking about. And my young friend, the host of the

evening was giving it his best shot, "aaaaah, think I can
rent that down at "BLOCKDUMPSTER?"...."and what was
    the name of it again?"
"Orange" I said, "just ask for ORANGE."

Guy next to me had heard enough. "You know I've seen you
    in here
before, whatyamean Orange, Orange what? Oranges are fruit
just like you are, you fucking windy old weirdo."
"Nah," bartender interjects dumping my ashtray, "Orange is
just a color, not my favorite one at that." Woman next to
me dismisses the entire discussion with a hiss, "and you
don't know your ass from an Orange hole in the ground."

Subject gets dropped. Hockey game ends in a tie
in overtime. Artists take down their paintings. Poet
disappears into a pitcher of beer. Dinner crowd is
already home asleep in front of the tube.

Owner of the bar walks in.
We pass as I'm walking out.
He asks "Hey, how ya doing?"
"Not sure," I go, "but Samuel Beckett would be proud."
Owner yells after me as I walk out the door,
"Now don't you fucking start with me!!"

4/97

REPORT FROM THE DYSFUNCTIONAL WORLD

Everyone keep their distance
until you get your reply
Soft eye soak in fear and gutless inaction.
Lost in the dessert of simple desert.
Too much sand bag dune fake out "Oyver butel"

But make an effort
so all your best intentions can be invalidated.
By our inattention and opulence in absentia,
and judged reason for huge jury, clear perfect perjury or
otherwise the ineffectual loose bowls of being under oath.

She sauntered in the bar;
sure of herself, as far as it went
suggesting, "I am a whirlwind of dysfunction
and you are my emotional pack mule."

Everyone looked in different neutral corners
finding no beast of Bourbon
searched for frame of reference,
and critical precedent for general easement.

Chemical dependence would be a sort of preferred
problem solving technique in lieu of that hard core
asshole that insisted upon being difficult and displaying
perplexing facial expressions and tone of voice in some
vague way suggested that they had actually lived to some end
How annoying!
Let my world shrink into a hard round ball of my
own limited sphere.
Bounce me.
But only so far.
And be done with it.

91

FRAGMENT OF A FORGOTTEN LETTER

I wish I was back there with you still
when the summer night showed July of 1971
Tall wheat went shoulder height
golden waves broke ranks
and ran across the morning heat
Your head I saw nod once and cock on an angle
So that your eyes were full of my foolish face.

You went to Canada with your family
and wished you were here in my arms
instead of having the soft inner thighs
of your legs sweaty stuck to the vinyl
of your dad's backseat with your underpants
riding up your bottom.

You were the beautiful child who wrote
me long letters.
I remember re-licking the glue on the flap
knowing your tongue had been there.
Mornings of thick curly brown strands
passing over my face to awaken the sensation
of cheek press upon cheek at first light
on the front porch on third street.

And I believe the line went,
"I wish I was back there
with you in the Movie Theatre
at 6:30 before the doors opened
and we were up in the lodge in
cool shadowy corners necking
on the carpet that smelled like
stale smoke and stranger's heels
and stale popcorn and I'm getting
pretty wet and the world couldn't
get at me there yet."

90

VAPOR MAP

Again you in that dream last night
driven from my bed I fell asleep in the gutter
with a hard intersection pillow
next to me asleep mutter in black hair as dark nest.

In the nest was this blank page left open on a desk in
the house last night with the pen left in the middle.
With a glance over my shoulder I thought with a glare,
I sure wish something soon would show up there.

Next morning on the way out the door to take the garbage
out, I noticed the page was full of writing.
I shrugged and stuck the black bags at the edge of the curb
hoping for routine disposal.

Then I went back to bed.
To try and finish that dream.
Where I was certain I would be allowed to read what
was written on that page in the back room.

The two women were back there.
Doing things to each other while watching my eyes.
It turned out to be a coitus interrupts blink.
Prior to any climax; children peeked, authorities warned
phones rang and the door knocked.

I reached for the ringing and it woke me up.

When I came back into the room,
they were both dressed.
As I suggested that they didn't give up and stop
pulling on their sweaters the dream ended.

Alone in acres of cool white sheets with a hard on
I went out the back room pulling thick oily black
pubic hairs from between my teeth to read what was on the
page. It was empty again.

I heard my voice say, "What are we going to do about this?"
She answered, "Nothing, besides, you're so good at it."

Dec 91

PLIERS

We sat in the bar.

He said, "gimme a beer."

He was holding his jaw taut.

"Most people," I remarked, "keep a stiff upper lip."

He was not amused, however, he attempted a grin without
moving his mouth and asked, "Ever try home dentistry?"

"Nah," I shrugged, "me, I'm a coward, even when it comes to
facing

the professionals, gas or no gas, I've got a fault line in
my mouth that makes the San Andreas look like a relief map
on that guy's face over there."

They turned their necks to see a huge young man in a muscle
shirt, beer belly across the front it read, "Woodstock
was a mistake-kill them all." He looked like he shaved with a
hedge hog four times a day. He was a bottle of dry light
staring at them.

"So what's your point?" he asked.

"Well, it's really all just a matter of time."

They laughed. They were all easily amused.

"Yeah," he said "Check this out."

He opened his mouth and there was a black gap, that
I didn't care to look at too closely.

"What happened?"

"I yanked that mother out, I just couldn't stand it
anymore. Yesterday afternoon at work we were putting a room
over a goatshead in fourth ward, I grabbed a pair of
pliers and a dish towel and I....."

I interrupted. "You're not really gonna tell me this, are you?"

Sure as shit, if I can have done this, the least you
can do is give a listen," he snapped. "Do you have any
        fuckin idea
what my jaw feels like right now."
"O.K......sure go right ahead....I guess."
I already knew what was coming.
He did. With the pliers. Wrapped in the dish towel.
No. It didn't just come out right like that.
Best he could do at first was make the goddamn thing hurt so
bad that he had to keep yanking tighter and twisting
till after a good ten minutes it was still dangling thickly by the
root nerve and after about nine fat fingers of Old Grand
Dad. Shit, by now there is blood and whiskey all over the
kitchen, I thought Randy was gonna throw up.
I thought now or never. Man, that last snap of gum and flesh
went off like a meat cleaver that triggered a twenty two
lined not up your asshole but in your mouth.

"How ya feeling now?" I asked.
"About the same, but I think I beat the Dentist outta about
300 bucks...."

"So now you think you're ahead, $300 to the good."

"Right," I said. Let's drop it I thought.
I couldn't help it. I had to ask,
"You mean to say with all that pain you caused yourself by
doing what you did, you helped yourself out in some way?
You really think it's better to make the fire in
your mouth be at the mercy of your own hand?"
"Hey, don't forget about the money," He thin lipped this out.
"Just Western Unioned the 300 bucks to my old Latino flame
down in Brooklyn, she was in some jam I guess, ... I'll
probably never see the money again."
"Or the tooth either", I remarked.

I thought: "Here's my pal full Vietnam Vet., P.O.W., nearly
    offed in the
jungle, shot at, wept over, given up for dead, with a mouth full
of mutant wasps and hornets in the inside of his jaws and
with a face full of that calmly wires off three hundred
creeping Charlies to old girl friends.
We drank more beer.
His jaw loosened somewhat.
About midnight, in walks his Latino Lover and her sister
who is even more strikingly attractive.
She throws those long slim brown arms around his neck
and purrs, "Hiya baby. Thanks."

I looked at them, then I looked at the sister.
She smiled very nicely.
I slugged down my beer in high white foam
and headed out the door.

My pal yelled, "Hey where the fuck are you going?"

I shouted over my shoulder, "Pliers."

July 91

SUNDAY NIGHT OF THE HEART

(For R.A.M.)

While I was working at this job, where they didn't
hire me, teaching teenagers lessons that I never learned,
defining words I half understood, in a class that was not
mine, I fell in love with a girl, half my age, I went over
to the window as the classroom went silent, I got lost....

.....in the Sunday night of the heart. Full moon as a
pock parked stooge, slung like a bone tinted tombstone in
blue and black. A few frizzy haloed ropes of vapor hung all
hopes by the neck, until the very nature of the night was
the snap of the till lip. The charmless chime of a celestial
cash register ringing up a big "No sale" for the heart.

There is the sound from a pay phone ringing down
the corner, the next block over, underneath an empty
street light. The persistent echo is a reoccurring
hallucination, of a red shark whose true ruby tail lights
don't search the night for him anymore.

So now it's the deep six stroll on a splintered
bulkhead where an unsteady soul is walking on the dock
in the dark looking to avoid the weak plank, that cracked
stringer, while the inky black water
chopping below almost looks like a good solution.

Somebody take this wrecking bar out of my hands
and point me back towards the shore.

"I waltz all over your planet and I'll kick dirt
where I want."

That's what Monk says. I like it so much that I slap him
on the back so hard that there is a POP in the air. But
the bravado doesn't last. Soon the mumbling starts. And the
eyes of the night get blasted inward with rum and orange
juice, that turns so sour and very yellow and wastes your
time while a set of wounded eyes asks, "How my doing?"
And you reply, " I don't know, what are you trying to do?"
Shrugging we both turn to watch a drunk play the cigarette
machine like it was a cross between a jukebox and a one
arm bandit. Then the bell went off, louder this time...

....and it brought me back to the window, and the
blackboard and the class, who wished that the teacher would

snap out of it and talk to them some more. They liked it
when he talked to them and not the night, at this job he
never got, wishing they were all his students, using words
he half understood, teaching lessons, he never learned,
and that girl half his age he once fell in love with,
all knew better, but would have to wait years for the
Sunday night of their heart.

10/84-3/95

DREAMBEERS

(For K.)

Dreambeer haunted he looked down at his glass and said,
"Dammit, how come he always has beer clouds in his bottle?"
Floating in that white cotton frosty creamy froth.
He looked down at his glass and his beer looked
like lukewarm flat rat piss that had been stepped on...twice.

There was that voice lost in the wire again.
It sounded like you could pull his face through.
His favors asking with a soft grin hissing
promises of return and spin
and you wanted in to his letters
to have at each word
only to enunciate each syllable
look it up over and over
and hear the sound of the words alive in the ear.

"Dammit, how come he always has beer clouds in his eyes?"
Only on nights like these. When the world feels stiff, sure
weary and predictable.
Even the jukebox can't swallow the coins fast enough.
"Watch the way he drinks."
He shoots the yeast back
into his throat hard and fast.

"How did he ever remember my number?"

June 90

UNITED STATES OF DISNEYLAND

Please extinguish all smoking materials here.
Gates open at eight.
Please extinguish all brains and grey matter here.
Gates open at eight
Thank you, have a nice day, have a nice stay.
Please step right this way;
Please extinguish all independent imaginations here.
Please stay in line keep your seats gates will open at eight.
Please extinguish all individuality here.
Let's open the big gate and masturbate
because it's the United States of Disneyland.

Say "Hello" to Mickey....why he's got a little white hand
for you to hold...in the other, there's a fist
and pal, I think, this Mickey has a nice long list
over who's allowed in and who gets the boot.
The streets are magic; the streets are crime free
all clean and authentically detailed with para-military
students doing their workouts or was that work overs with the
original cast fresh from K-Mart dressed in Beatle boots
ready to answer all your questions, as long as there good
useful positive questions. Whoops look at the time, Gotta go
and have a beer with Goofy.

Old Walt's on ice.
Seven little dwarfs blowing down a little crack.
Sorry sir... there's no smoking here or there
Good old Pinocchio with his nose on fire
Don't be alarmed.... it's all under control
just do what you do best.....sit there....be entertained, stare.

And it's "Hi ho hi ho" it's off to detention center we go
"Hi ho hi ho" we caught you with some blow
"Have you seen our Ministry of Truth Exhibit?"
Right over here near the Epcot center...no? Well then
let's slip on these plastic handcuffs and go have a peek.
Let's dance over there with the bunnies and raccoons and the
weasels and the prancing rats and goose stepping Jackals.
It's the new dance of the 90's,
a test a day keeps the thoughts away.
Then you can keep your job...body slamming carped foam
on magic mountain right next to the magic containment

compound and enchanted social disease holding area.
Hey look, after my drug test, AIDS test, V.D. test,
Cholesterol screening, I'm free for the rest of the day.
Let's go and find Goofy and have a beer. Again.
And tonight it will be nothing but dwarfs till dawn,
All of them..Sneezy, Happy, Snappy, Pushy, Shovey, Pully,
Doc, Daryl, Bashful, Grumpy, Worthless, Distasteful,
     Spiteful,
Lucky, Drooly, Juicy, Tragically.....
Why the dirty little bunch of Jerk-offs.

And it's zip a dee do da, zip a de day
Snow white fucked Sleeping Beauty's Prince behind her back
He was a stock broker by day.
Zip a de do da, zip a de day.
My O my, what a blessed toy town lust and greedy display.

New theme music nightly. Dancing Corporate elephants
trampling fields of yellow petunias...holding hands dancing
on the third world to a little Dixieland everyone in red
striped jackets and clean white modest dresses
eating lowfat, high fiber, pulverized vanilla ice cream.
Doing what the fuck they're told.

Oh steel silos.
Miles of grey monoliths, no money, no food tickets.
Just little playgrounds with iron statues of Stromboli
that look like Stalin.
But not to worry,..we'll have a parade with floats and bands
and tanks and missiles and food riot squads...and then we'll
have a show and you can be in it. IN FACT, YOU ARE THE
SHOW!! Just sit up there in the witness stand. We want to
ask you a few harmless questions... You've been bad mouthing
the Mouse again....right? All those snide comments about
having to do Mickey's march...walk a mile in his cartoon
shoes..Live his little cartoon life. You're just some bitter
paranoid old fool aren't you? What is all this bullshit
you spout about deadly subliminal oppression? Who says that
it's the end of Individuality, Expression and Imagination?
Now it's your turn to recant... To confess to everything...
You still think like some goddamn teenager dolled up in
spando stretch pants and cockatoo hair listening to that
dangerous evil rock music that is the devils voice on earth
and sounds like Donald Duck quacking with his
        nuts squeezed
in an interrogation room vice. Confess...confess...
Please watch your monitors as the all new 24hr. Disney
Channel pops into the network feeds hourly and it's
        our leader,
    our spokesman, our protector, the spiritual fountain head,
        so cute
    so small, so black and white...why we can hardly see his

little ears over the podium as the stage hand gets him
a soap box and there he is smiling, laughing, his eyes are
twinkling and with the white gloves, he makes a sweeping
gesture..
 "WHY HIYA EVERYBODY I-AM-THE-SOMEBODY-
WITH-THE-MASTER-PLAN-FOR-ALL-THE-
        NOBODIES......."

So when you wish upon a star,
it had better be more than with Goofy in a bar.
Please...Extinguish your basic rights here.
Thank you for not smoking...
Thank you for not thinking...
Thank you for not caring....
Thank you for being kinder and gentler...
Thank you for being full of WONDER...
Thank you for all the POWER.
Gates will be closing at eight...
Here in the United States of Disneyland.

87

WHAT A HOT HORSE REMEMBERS

The second cigarette that Hot Horse lit that morning
made him dizzy. He needed to sit. He weaved over to the
scuffed black plastic TV chairs and slouched down,
let out a sigh, farted gently, winced at the ensuing
bouquet and sneaked quick guilty looks hoping no one
was close enough to notice.
The screen of the set was smudged with greasy finger
prints. The grimy opaque lifeless surface threw back a
dreadful distorted reflection.
"Bad mirror," thought Hot Horse and dug for a couple of
quarters to shut it up. The screen blinked to grey image.
Healthy looking teenagers were chewing diet gum and
cleaning A-K 47s and singing. Hot Horse was
grateful the sound was down. Trouble was that both the
greasy finger prints and his own face were still visible.
This made Hot Horse want to throw up. Instead he butted
the smoke partially in the ash can, so it was doing a slow
smolder, in a slim thread that snaked straight up. He closed
his eyes and tried to nod. He was thinking about yesterday.
It had been a long day for Hot Horse. Rising about eight,
he had reheated a couple of slices of last week's pizza
and after a little consideration, he went back to bed.

Sometime around noon, as the room grew hotter and more
stuffy, a particularly powerful and pungent gas problem,
woke him half way, with the suggestion that a feta cheese

/egg salad sandwich exiled twenty one days in a zip-lock
baggie had just been ice-picked in the room.
What had brought him around fully to semi-consciousness was
the sound of some loud snarling down below in the next yard
over. Hot Horse tumbled off the mattress on the floor and
crept on all fours, over to the window by the stove and
peeked around the curtains. A woman, about sixty, crowned
with platinum blond hair and grey black roots was screaming
at the rear opening on the garage,
"Just who IN HELL do YOU think I AM!!??" Hot Horse
dared a little deeper peek. She appeared to admonishing
a 73 Camaro. If her impassioned rant and berating tone
was directed toward the direction of the two young men,
with the dirty surgical masks on, spray painting the orange
Camaro red, they gave little impression they were aware of
her presence. The added fury of the air-compressor might
have explained this, but it was by no means drowning her out.

There was a lot of bad air being expelled down there as well.
"Maybe they are used to it," thought Hot Horse.
As he was about to crawl back
to the mattress losing interest, another car
pulled into the driveway. It was a battered blue Pinto,
with the front shock springs busted. The finish on the
exterior was peeling off in long ragged strips.

It reminded Hot Horse of a potato peeled by a blind man,
either that or the Pinto had just barely made it through
a partially difficult re-entry into the earth's atmosphere.
It was hot down in the driveway. The sunlight beat down on
everything like a second skin of Verathane. Out of the
beat space/shopping center shuttle climbed two
heavy set women. One was bigger than the other.
"That must be the leader," thought Hot Horse.
She wore dark blue stretch pants, pink slippers, with the

backs broken, her dirty calloused heels protruded nakedly like dried sweet potatoes. Up top she sported a tight fitting striped polo shirt with a picture of a Garth Brooks on the front, while on the back, spelled out in glitter was the name "Tammy." Tammy had a roll of fat, which was a good four inch bulge in diameter that hula-hooped her lower stomach which was set adrift her hips. It was just about the size of her breasts, which hung flatly.

It looked like she was wearing twin
mildly deflated inner tubes
around her torso and chest.

"Good," thought Hot Horse, maybe they'll leave and go to the beach."

Tammy's companion was perhaps
about twenty years younger.

She was just as large, but much more smoothly tapered.

She merely looked like a distended old WW II torpedo.

They both smoked extra long filter cigarettes, freshly lit.

Hot Horse decided that the art of synchronized smoking was not dead and these folks obviously had practiced.

Tammy was chewing gum with some vigor. It made the
extra long
filter More protruding from the corner of her mouth
twirl the figure eight. Just another example of hard work and dedication paying off.

The younger woman had a harlequin pair
of sunglasses and a massive beehive hair-do that was covered with an aqua blue fishnet.

Hot Horse could smell them from down there.

After a brief deliberation, all three women started to
yell at the rear end of the red Camaro.

The two men kept spraying the car. Acknowledgment,
at present did not seem to be forth coming. Hot Horse drew away from the window and realized that life had come to this.

Hot Horse opened his eyes. Had he dozed off?
The screen was black and his tired face was back
on the screen. Was it all a dream or nightmare?
Hot Horse yawned, stretched and scratched, still groggy
and dizzy. He looked around eager for something to watch.
He was out of quarters. Next aisle over were a young couple
of lovers, eating Ho-Ho's, doing a flesh pretzel, as one gave
the other a hickey, between bites, the other was watching the
chair mounted TV. Next Hot Horse had his attention
arrested by a man of average height in a black leather
fringed jacket. He was giving the change
machine hell for eating his buck and not spitting out coins.
A security guard was watching the man closely.
After a big paw of air, Tex straightened up, cocked the
midnight shadow cowboy hat a little more erect and drawled,
"Welllll......I'll be dammmmnned."
The angle of his hat and shoulders were perfectly
perpendicular to each other. Hot Horse deduced that Tex
must have been a mighty strong cowpoke to be able to
walk around with such a big wooden chip perched
up top.

He had seen lots of these types: ageless, fire-hydrant
assed, a mud smudge of mustache (it looked like badly
penciled in Maybelline). The goose's ass hair on his chin
made him appear like a springtime hipster mule in heat.
The loud taps on his worn grey cowboy boots, (with tassels)
resounded as he walked away muttering obscene threats,
throwing murderous glances at anyone staring at him.
Tex strutted off into the locker-for-rent sunset,
his work here, obviously done.

The waiting room started to fill up. It was Easter week

and Hot Horse watched the suntan college girls on spring
break pass by in little groups of two or three, some holding
potted white lilies, looking like various flavors of pastel
tinted carpeted colored candy. In their wake they left a
clean, perfumed air that made Hot Horse feel vaguely soiled.

Now Hot Horse was depressed.
There was still another hour till his bus left.
Hot Horse thought about rising from the dead,
but he had already done that last week.

6/85-3/95

HOW TO MANAGE

Ever wonder how to manage?

Ever wonder how we all seem to manage?

Ever wonder what you would manage

if you could figure out how to manage it?

I was born the son of a movie manager. When I grew older
he used to let me fill in for him on his nights off. This
was how I learned to manage. This is where I learned to
manage. The theater was opened in 1938. It was a buffed
jewel stone of imageland. Thousands of individual bricks
inlaid in intricate patterns stood proud the edifice. The
marquee had an illuminating chaser system that glowed and
blinked orange and yellow brilliance in sequence. The
interior was a wild rich dance of flowered carpets, plush
deep red seats, opulent wall fabrics and soft mysterious
winking secret lights and shadows everywhere. Such was the
prime of the theater's life and many were the nights people
of the village waited in long lines to get in.

Now forty years later it stands empty. It leans slightly
to the side like an old white elephant with Alzheimers.
It has become like a Deco-desperado ghost hangar, where
the Zeppelins of showbiz Limbo past land just after
hours loaded with all the would be actors and actresses and
little known extras who sit around all night in the empty

theater discussing why their careers never made it. Before
first light the Zeppelin comes back to pick them all up and
they all go out for breakfast at diners that no longer exist.

The theater is always glad to see these visitors of
the night, let's just say that these long dead failed
performers remind the theater of when life was young and the
theater was in better shape. The years have taken their
toll. The weary, worn out wiring makes the house lights
blink in hot flashes and then dim during show times.
The huge proud curtain which used to part dramatically
to signal the start of the show and sadly slowly close in
a sweeping gesture of finality at the end of the night
hasn't made a move in years. This embarrasses the theater
to no end.

It's like having your zipper on your fly
open and broken all the time.

Upstairs in the projection booth, the operator still
burns carbon rods to show each reel of tonight's feature.
Sections of the lodge seats are roped because
the ceiling plaster is crumbling.

Tonight I'm sitting at the Manager's desk. I know this
office as well as it knows me. It watched me grow from a
child to a man. My father sat in this seat at the office
desk most of his adult life. The time he knew as a young man
blows into the office tonight like a forgotten
passenger of the Limbo Zeppelin who was left behind by
accident and now tries to hitch a ride on the cuff of the next out
bound July thunderstorm. Such was the passing of his years.
He met my mother in this place. She was the box-office lady.
She sold the tickets, punched the keys on the magazine of the
ticket machine. She was a honey haired hometown girl from a

large Irish/German family. He was a jet black haired guy
from out of town with a thin black mustache like a young
David Niven. At first, they used to steal shy glances at
each other through the little door between the Manager's
office and box office. It was 1947 and they were in
Show Business together. After the show they used to have
dates to go out for beers and soft shell crabs at a place
that has long since burned down to the ground.

So with that in the back of my mind, I always wear
a white shirt and thin black tie when I manage here.

The lights blink and flash and I hear a voice calling
me from the foyer. So I walk out to the candy stand, which
is closed at this late hour but after looking hard and long
at the hopeful young faces of the little boys, I re-open the
stand to give them Frozen Milky Ways or Sweet-Tarts. I must
seem like so much slow motion to their eager fresh candy
hungry eyes. I like telling them to be quiet in a serious
low voice. With their hands full, they disappear and I
wonder if they will ever know anything as well as I do every
brick in this theater. I'd match my own ghosts here tonight
with any phantoms left to whisper in hushed tones that echo
in the ladies room.

One of my ghosts plays on the floor of the office.

That's me at about five. Another ghost hangs out in the
alley next to the theater smoking a reefer. That's me at
about seventeen. If you were to walk all the way down to the
front of the theater you could go behind the huge projection
screen. You can climb up twenty feet or better in the air
on the fire escape behind it. I've sat upon the top steps of
the fire escape behind the white snowy screen with
thousands of tiny holes to watch the backward images of

the night's features pass through and be
projected onto myself like the wildest suit of clothes in the
world. One night you might wear the skyline of Nevada.
The next Sean Connery's smirk or air support from THE
LONGEST DAY.

Soon the show will be over. I know how to lock it all
up from routine, observation and memory. I'm waiting for
the credits to roll. I'm in the lobby looking out across the
street at the Italian restaurant. She used to come out in
her white waitress dress to wave at me. Her skin smelled
like every good and greasy temptation that ever came out
of a kitchen. Even that was awhile ago now.

The late crowd is on the exit. I watch their faces
for signs of satisfaction or disapproval. It just looks like
they all had popcorn, whether they wanted it or not. I wonder
what the faces of those exiting reflected when the theater had
first opened. Well the show is breaking, this is how to manage:

1. Show up early.

2. Reassure the Owners (if they call)

3. Joke with the Ushers.

4. Never get pissed at the patrons.

5. Passes for Friends. Scalp the acquaintances.

6 Remember your keys to get in.

7. Drop hot ashes on the desk.

8. Keep all beer as cold as possible and December

Holy in the ice cream freezer. (This is because
You never know who might show up.)

9. Look out the lobby doors through the glass
And sigh deeply if they never show.

10. Pin back the lobby doors.

11. Pin back the rest room doors.
(Either take a deep whiff or hold your breath)

12. Check all the panic bars on the exits.

13. Wave at the shadows that refuse to leave.

14. Walk down the empty aisles kicking popcorn
Cups on the way down to extinguishing the air.

15. Take a walk across the stage in front
Of the wide, white blank screen of the vacated
Theater and thank everyone for coming.

16. Flip on the answering machine in the office.

17. Turn out the house lights slowly one by one
Saying each one's name as you do.

18. Put on the anti-crime light in the lobby.

19. Before slamming the office door with a
Resounding thud make certain you didn't
Leave your keys on the desk.

20. Listen to the sound of your footsteps echoing
    In the lobby as you walk out, re-check the
    Latch pins on the front doors. Lock it up.

21. Go out and get a cold one.

This then is how I manage.
By the way, how do you manage?

10/83-9/94

THE DENTIST OF TIME

(For T.N.)

Have the good sense to recognize this moment.
This second of calm, this inkling of peace
where trains run on time; there is heat in your
bedroom at midnight; with spaghetti freshly knotted
warm bellies full.
Pick up this jewel of this second and hold it up to the
light to let the prisms of rainbow wonder cascade into
your eyes. Take this moment; blow life into it; caress it
to your cheek, acknowledge it; rejoice and take heed of
your little weary steps on your path that is your
certain pathway to aspiration and stars or perhaps you
see dark woods ahead or amber open land;
Remember:

> The Dentist of time is coming;
> is coming.

Eat the Lean Cuisine
Sigh and sing along with, "Oh, what a beautiful morning."
With Harry and Paula and 5th detention group chorus of
the Illinois State Correctional Shock Camp.
Then it's off to your career. Commute feeling "good about
yourself." Safe and secure that reality is so well
proportioned and benign.
Tool the Lumina smugly; have a little nod on your daily
train; glance drowsy eyed out the window with vague dreams

and desires of power, opulence and self-assured position
and dominance. Indulge now....because..

The Dentist of time is coming.

is coming.

Worship in the glittering vacant towers of authority.
Humble yourself at the feet of Corporate might,
Kiss those toes till the sun goes down then it's off
to your health spa to experience your personal best
while sneering or lusting at all the flesh you don't
desire or wish for a crack at. Take a crisp cold shower
and end your day at the local tinsel and shadow disco
to gyrate your pelvis into the deafening nothingness.
Take cocaine; better not take cocaine; have a drink
oh, no more drinks for me. Drive blind drunk or select your
designated conscience chauffeur while sucking on a
shaker of salt; OH YES, MORE TEQUILA!!!!
It really doesn't matter because

The dentist of Time is coming

is coming

The dentist of Time is coming.

Mousse that hair, strip outta the slip.
What a great commercial. You're the new Fox vehicle.
It's called "Unnatural Acts." And you're on location
in your closet; O.K. out of the closet in the front
yard. In front of the neighbors in the back yard.

Piss out the window of a second story flat to prove
you're an "elevated achiever"

Or across the parking lot after
midnight to exert your womanhood.
Fill the condoms with snow caps, Nonpareils or gummy
little power rangers, fruit and fiber juicy snakes,

Let your fashion sense, your passion for fashion give
a warm fuzzy fuckin illusion of freedom...
                        Because the Dentist
                            is coming.
                                The Dentist of
                                time is coming.

Oh, sit there o most blessed be smirking youth.
For you there still is time to start screaming,
"Not me! Not me!"
All those half awake omnipotent twenty year
old experts have been marketed right out of their
identities. What's my line has been replaced by what's
my target group. And there looks like nothing but a
bullseye in all your faces.
Who's buying this whole Melrose race?
What of the blase? The stodgy. The imperial smugness.
Those sunglasses hung around your neck
like a hangman's noose of arrogance. Emphatically
denying any vision, embracing the diminishing
personal freedoms of a post-industrial, pre-world
economic collapse, the new bar code rules
of order and conduct for safe passage to full fledged
adult toyland of perpetual adolescent gratification.
Ken's dream house car career never looked so good. Such
        a sure
thing. And Barbie. The smooth creamy plastic skin between
her credit card legs is pure Beverly Hills teen animation.
                                Never guessing the
                                Dentist of time is coming.

Somewhere on another day in a grey room of future tense,
in either corporate luxury or Fellahin poverty; remote
control or greasy frying pan stain on the kitchen wall
Di-chron polyester with care-free Herculon or thread bare

underwear splattered plastic couch covers.
You will hear the footsteps from down the hallway,
and then up the stairs and your door will explode into
fragments and in will come the men in grey or black or
brown with shouldered truncheon and they will straddle you
side by side and pick you up by the armpits, so that your
feet don't quite touch the ground and twitch like freshly
run over rabbit's paws.
And then the men will say, "You have an appointment
                                    with the Dentist.
                                    "The time is here."

                                              87/94

THE POET LINE

Hello, you have reached Poet phone. If you are calling
from a touch tone phone please press one. If you are
calling from a rotary phone please stay on the line
and your call will be answered by the first available
poet who will read you a carefully prepared sonnet designed
to encourage you to stop living in 1964 and embrace modern
communication devices before it's too late. If you fail to do
this the poet will then wail, shriek and flip out at you
because you never change, you never listen and you always do
this. The line will be disconnected. And you be left alone
holding the receiver by yourself. So all alone. Left alone to
wonder what the hell is ever going to happen to you if
you don't get a hold of yourself.

If you are looking for advice on how to get your dismal,
second rate derivative drivel published please press two.

If you are a published poet and wish to have someone to
brag to and smugly bully everyone else in the room, making them
feel stupid for trying to create in your omnipotent
presence press three.

If you are on a speaker phone and are having a small
get together and have had a few and desire something for low
grade entertainment to dismiss and sneer at collectively
as ridiculous bargain basement pathos press four.

If you are ready to kill yourself and need a few lines
of hope and encouragement and sympathy please seek
     professional
help, everybody here feels like that too and doesn't want
to hear it again and doesn't know what the fuck to tell
you either.

If you have called in search of truth, beauty, grace or
wisdom, press five.
Then hold your phone receiver out at arm's
length away from your ear. The howls of laughter tend to be
rather loud and could blow out your eardrum.

If you are waiting for something to happen in your life
and don't feel you can last much longer and don't know
where to turn, what to feel or whom to trust, press six.
You'll be put on hold. We'll get back to you.
If you wish to be put in contact with other local poets
in your immediate area so you can form one of those little
self-important inbred writers
workshops where everyone snacks
off each other's poetic feces laden ditties and strangles to
death any real fresh creativity, please press seven.

All those in love with the sound of their own voice and who wish
to record a few hundred pages of their latest epic, you may
press eight for rate schedule and have a major credit card
number handy.

Press the number nine for additional menu.
You have pressed nine....please hold.

Dear caller...you have pressed nine for more choices.
There are no more choices. Fresh out. Can we ask you a rather
personal question? Why did you call this number in the first

place? Did you really expect to be able to pick out some
trite flat saccharin all purpose numbness that brainwashes
while it mollifies the shallowness in those TV ears?
This poet line is different.
We kick ass and take names.
But....we always forget them afterwards.
So you want more choices, Hah?
Well, who the hell doesn't?
Your crummy taste limits our choices.
We'd like a few more things to choose from.
Like how about a few open minds.
Some individuals from time to time.
A voice or two raised for some good end.
A publisher bat shit enough to pull our stuff in print.
An urge to create instead of always consuming.
Did you ever wonder what you expected from your life
      anyway?
When did you reach the point, where you expected to be
able to access a little poetry in the same fashion
you check your credit card balance?
Well pal, here's your credit report according to us here
at the poet line.
You're at risk. In your habits and the blind fashion you
conduct the dull music of your days.
There's no spark. When's the last time you shone inside
like gaudy carnival from afar on a summer's evening?
What did you hear in the last twenty four hours that moved
you to reflect in sound the marvel of the senses?
Why does the light fade so softly in your deafness?
What spirit sleeps now and when was the last time it

rose up in you like a tidal wave?
When was the last time you could not contain your joy?

Thank you for calling the Poet Line.
Please hang up now.
Go live with a little grace.
Some vibrancy.
And for crying out loud stop using
convenient, instant gratification
contrivances to define
your vague adolescent desires.
This is going to cost you.
We made our impression.
Wait till you get the bill.

11/93

HOLIDAY FOR
NEUROTICS

Some say it starts at Thanksgiving
the same ones who mutter under their breath
as the mailman walks away, "I pity the next sorry
bastard asks how my TURKEY day was!"

"Hey....this was my big year I managed to completely
defrost the MSG pigeon and not cook the giblets
in the paper packet inside the gutted body cavity."

And the best part are all the relatives and in-laws
in the living room the kitchen, the bathroom, the telephone.
The measured, inquisitional, hyper calm voice of your mother
in-law on the line. You know the one who looks at you like
you are a cross between Judas and little Charlie Manson.
She has been extremely patient with you. After all she knows
you're sure to screw up sooner or later.
The Uncles who after you ask for some advice can hardly
contain the merriment sparkling in their eyes saying,
"you mean to tell me, it's taken you this long to realize
that you've been barking up the wrong tree for so long,
why it's a wonder you can even still talk with all the
dead leaves stuck down your throat."

The holiday neurotic
and it's only the beginning.
The day after "Turkey Day"
is, of course, "Shopping Day."
The popular culture starts winding up the elastic
band of consumption, twisting tighter, smaller knots
of blind wild product orgy. Perfect.
There may be a need for safe sex.
But safe shopping? Nah. Never.

Then PBS will start it's "A Wonderful Life" loop.
George Bailey in tears on the bridge in the snow
24 hrs. a day. Clarence Oddbody and George Bailey
being booted out of Nick's as the bartender snarls,
"Listen this is a bar for men who want to drink hard
Liquour to get drunk fast and we don't need any characters
coming in here given the joint ATMOSPHERE.
Now do I makemyself clear or do I need to slip
  you a knuckle sandwich for a convincer!!"
And for once you're not left in tears on the couch torn by the
realization you wished the angel just might blow
it. George would either drown or the whole town wouldn't
show up in a spontaneous gesture of good will to pay
off his debts. And off old George would be hauled to the
can on Christmas Eve as Donna Reed and the kids all sob.
It wouldn't be a wonderful life but dammit to hell it
would be real life.

And, of course, there's the Christmas music.
Deck the Halls, hit the deck over in Automotive.
K-Spotted Wal-Mart-ed waltzing to the sleigh bells
in the snow in the parking lot.
It's on the radio, "Hit the deck with boughs of folly."
OH ATM, OH ATM, OH ATM, OH ATM
Why were the greedy store owners pulverizing those

Carols to death? The songs had long since lost any meaning.
Now they were the obligatory soundtrack to the
mandatory consumption. It wasn't fair. It wasn't even music
anymore. You could not escape. You could not win.
The more reverent the sentiments the more absurd your
surroundings became. Away in a manger in the
small appliance department. Standing in a line that snakes
back all the way back past stationery through women's
underwear to the little town of Bethlehem.
The endless march of faces.
Everybody looking like their own banal Commercial induced
product choice.
They looked like programs teetering on cancellation.
The droves.
It was the Bataan death march of December.
The vacant eyes. The jaws slowly working the gum.
Here come the eager. Here come the weary.
There go the satiated. There go the shopping Maul zombies
numbing, stumbling across the tile while, Grand Ma, got
run over by a Reindeer as done by Soul Asylum, blast out
overhead from the invisible P.A.'s.
And your present this year?
Why it's the realization you're just another one of them.
No different. Worse really. You feel like this.
Shit! At least they're happy...er...content...ah...well
adjusted to this convoluted contrived artificial cathedral.
So shaddup and face Mecca.
It's that way. Just to the left over near Sears.

Ducking into a bar. You sigh. Order up. And your shoulders
slump. What the hell is the matter with me anyway?

I feel like this all year round.
Not just at Christmas time.
And in a blue funk you start a conversation with a stranger.
You both commiserate. Yeah, it's so commercial. Yeah, it's a
big pain in the ass. Yeah, ain't like it used to be.
So you tell your stories of the past Christmases.
And your new friend tells his.
Then you both get real quiet.
Sit there elbow to elbow.
Soon it's time to go.
And as you shake hands and catch that something in each
other's eye, while wishing seasons greetings, walk away
feeling a little better thinking, "Christ, at least I ain't as
bad off as that crazy bastard. Merry Christmas to you too,
pal, you're gonna need it."

Dec. 92-93

FOR T. MONK

Coming along the Hudson
that April afternoon. I sat
in a newspaper nest gathered for price
of purchase in Albany with her sigh
as she saw a lot of this sort of incidental
train face, in a hurry for the N.Y. papers
or cigarettes in forty seconds time, some
looked like it would be great to just leave this
boring little dinky job and go with them. Anywhere.
And it always made her wonder who or where or why?
His grave battered manners and stately eloquence at the
pit stop at the county fair's annual demolition derby.
Some passengers just left you shaking your head at the
back end of a train.

Coming along the Hudson
that April afternoon I perched in a swivel
lounger in the refreshment car. Outside the
water of the river bore stars and glistened;
Inside the inevitable redhead furrowed her
yellow brown brows; worry creases to beat and
please don't bat those baby blues this afternoon,
you see she was reading "Fiction."
Or at least trying to understand the scarcity of it.
Mr. Lipman never gave his name, rather relaxed,
his business over for the week. He had the easy talk
going back down to the Bronx. Home. Crack Sermack.
The local hoodlums didn't bother him, in 1964 or now.

"I had shot a boy years ago...nothing too bad... ruined him
for life, ... if you can understand what I mean..."
His palms outstretched in gesture, "Of course, it's
the only way you have to deal with all Nishgutnicks."

This Thursday afternoon in 1990
with April able to still spring for this thread of memory.
Life and spirit turning in perpetual spin out of one tunnel
and into the next diminished shadow door.
A season full with a sudden still gentle
heart, easy demure and a quiet life lived
in an brief desert of sensation.

Coming along the Hudson;
we spoke of how it seemed women were

bigger these days. Then which bridge was which;
and wouldn't it be nice to have someone
good to come home to.
Look at that river begging a small boat and just fish
out of it.
Mrs. Marlow's heart valve, "They wanted to put a
pig's valve in." She giggled at seventy miles and years.
"But I told them that wouldn't be Kosher."

Lipman came back with,
"You know, they can hook you up with
microwaves to the telephone in your doctor's office to
monitor your heart. Mrs. Marlow blushed and said, "Oh my,
what if you get a wrong number?" And you're thinking "Geez
these people talk nice, how come you can't do that?"
Maybe it's because these people belong to another time
and you are so much a product of your own.
The ease and Pullman of Wolf's trains; the railroad of the
other October earth; passion and wonder on the pass in

split seconds. Seventy years for them. Soon the coach
went quiet, except the din of motion sliced sun shafts
down the car and over the faces like dominos falling in
sequence. But didn't we all sway and gently rock down the
rails toward Grand Central? If we could all keep our
mouths shut and eyes closed it could be any train, on any
year, anytime.
As long as it was a train where the sandy haired
blond, freckled Irish jewel with the thick throaty
brogue whispered, "Dublin, I'm going back to Dublin."
To which Mrs. Marlow says, "Whatcha say honey, I can't
        understand
yer?" The young girl lowering her eyes, embarrassed to
death, somewhat awed, shy and made very lonely by the
quickness of these New Yorkers, speaking in their own tongues
of so many things at once.

Coming along the Hudson
that April afternoon I sat
riding the Niagara Rainbow down from Buffalo
in a rat's nest of city dailies all open to the sports
pages. Thinking in terms of, if the train's on time,
I'll try it again. I'll risk the impetuous dash across
and under that city's face, debating with myself the
chances, the foolish madness of delightful deadly impulse.
To sneak up on one's self and merely attempt to dream the
deaf awake. To run into the vision's vortex of time and be
placed fully aware awake hungry thirsty. To grasp the mortal

reins of intent and yell, "GIDDIYAP. Open your arms heaven,
I want to sit in your lap." As the miles spilled
out upon each other we passed 125th street right before
the tunnel and I knew that it had come into the train
the city, my eyes desire fresh born again to run the
gauntlet. Pass under the towers of filth to flee to

the jewel in Queens again with a single minded purpose.
Then it's hitting the bricks, the feet alive on concrete
swimming out the blackness of the tunnel looking
for the way out. Blurring past luggage laden passengers
who move as if in a slower version of reality.
First things first. Hit the toll booth with a brown
paper bag of week old onion and submarine rolls
from the top of the ice box. Thinking Number 7.
Need to make deposit underneath the train station
sky toward sprawled beggars and excessed citizens.
Toward the tormented; Dante's walk ons, in a hyper
accelerated gait, he sat the bag down and said,
"Bread Man." From the floor came the recall, "Thank you,
bless you." And he threw over his shoulder, "Yeah, verily
it's cool and good too."

Out to Whitman's island in this time
rushing with the Wolfe's eyes
Awake in his only dream while all the others slumber.
Every cell for each their sentence to break,
his time approaching. The release in the sound of
the wish of the subway doors sliding open.
The sound of his cell door swinging open.
Then the footfall upon the concrete platform,
to run like he was twelve once more, when there
still was a good place to run to. The green
rucksack pounding at his shoulders, the late afternoon
sunshine and out by wind at his face, while the stadium
filled his eyes, the roar of the crowd grew in his ears.
In the wild sunshine of April spread across the familiar
parking lot, with the question asked at the gate, "Can I
still get in?", "Can I still buy a ticket?"
Syncopation here now had taken hold
over him and his actions.
The sound of the horn form a limo, the striding scalper,

on cue, barking, "Alright how many you need?"
"Just one", He lied and paid the price, with a slight
haggle and debate.
"HURRY up, MAN!" The scalper looking
warily over his shoulder, with the knowledge of timetables

and this stranger's face eager to get in.
Up the ramps, he felt the sensation of his legs
lifting himself toward his destination.
Contentment and vision fulfilled in cold hard reality.
Again dreaming the deaf awake in Queens.
Longing to give anything a point on a map.
a small slim needle with a round blue point on the end.
From point A to point B. The sweep of the cell door complete.
The feel of his ass in seat. Now in a huge open semi-circle
go the yellow swirl stiff wind pushing colors alive;
each speck with its own spark blending.
Then he sat in his place and became one of them.
The vision swayed in swells and eddying currents of sound.
He sat trying not to breathe so hard. It was true.
He wouldn't wake this time, till he was ready. His chest was
pounding as he forced himself to drink in every detail again
and again. The orange foul poles with white nets affixed like
sails. The structure that supported so much, so many, so
gracefully with sharp jutting symmetry in basic blue and
green. It was all very unbelievable and real. The clock had
stopped. He had pulled the plug. All was suspended. A
        moment
tacked down. Here. Hold me, it whispered. Press me to your
cheek. Go ahead, lean into that 94 per hour fastball, on the inside
corner, fouled off as flowing mosaic. The center cursor
gone like a homing pigeon. To touch other hands;
drunken young hungry fingers ready to be skinned and
scuffed over in the fight for a piece of it. All around
him they fought over it and as he watched it broke free

and bounced straight into his outstretched hands.
And he held it up in triumph and cheered at the top of
his lungs in the only crude way he knew.

And he had come along the Hudson;
that Thursday afternoon in April
longing for a look, to see, a song to sing
to be wide awake in this dream,
packing the notes of Monk,
And his child's face,
his Lover's heart
told him now to hold the sphere,
with the signature smeared,
in your grasp at last,
your fingers locked tightly
around the threads.
Here is your gift.

Here is your piece of it.
Your part in this,
that is yours.
Plant it deep in the heart's pocket,
and give it to anyone with the courage to ask.
This is your leaf, your stone, your door.

Back now to the grey tunnels and coming night.
A single figure in the first car on the number
7 back into Manhattan, with his head still swimming
in black sunset rails and blue sparks and signal
lights dropping red to green.
A brilliance along the black rail approaching.
That indescribable look locked upon his face,
his left hand buried hard in the pocket,
in his palm he held the ball.

April 90

SMALL TIME PRESS

NOT FOR EGG MEN ONLY: "HOW YA GONNA LIKE UM PRESS?"
APT #746 a-U, Court-16, Cockscomb Condominiums, Marshell Law, Calif. 11667

We are looking for the raw and uncooked aspects of expression. Around our press, we take the chicken or the egg business to heart. We have an on going debate/grudge over what came first. Cotton Mather or James Cotton? Smart toilets or wipies? In other words, we deal in philosophy. The word view of a small, however hardcore group of scrambled, fried, omeletted cowards/bitter eccentrics who never fail to make embarrassing public scenes over trifling matters in Super-Markets. A good day has the checkout girl in tears. We appear once or twice a year, either on shelf paper that arrives in empty Bounty rolls or handsome thermo-faxed, creamy pearl sheepskin, laser printed in bold two-point fuchsia dot-matrix classic. Publication length is anywhere from
50 to 100 pages long, press run approx. 6 to 1500.
(All this depends on what Geruard can dig up at
the local bar, in this small college town, where he is "pain-in-the-ass
in-residence poet-laureate." If this is the semester he finally runs out of young, naive, art/lit. majors to fleece for the press, then it could be some time before another press run. (After what we saw him with last night, wealthy coed in a little black outfit, with a reputation for a taste for protracted adolescence, it looks good for another year.)

Concerning submission; we have seen the hand writing on the wall. (And it stinks.) Please do not send us poems that are soft boiled in Pert.

We want real word food for hungry malcontents.

No whining wailing,

weeping, gnashing of teeth, no confessors' revisionist prattle, or Lego-deconstructionalist pikers.

(We get enough of this at home, and prefer to deal with one little Caesar at a time, and in person.) Also we don't care to hear from those with middle age laments over some tart down at the bar who refused to give him a tumble and did all his pals instead. Likewise save the pre-packaged robo-rhetoric stew/gruel ground out by some small time local deity/ham and eggs. We know what it is we want to see/hear. (Fruit of the Teflon.)

Cream of beat. You can eat it . Throw it. Leave it to harden in the sink. Hatch it. Cotton to it. Bully people with it. In short we want it to say "YOUNG MAN, IF I HAVE TO STOP THIS BAR, YOU ARE IN BIG TROUBLE!!

Advice to young poets; know how to separate the whites from the yolks before you write us. As a sample, we include an excerpt from Seth Drystales's "Remembering Perry Perdue (Frank's brother)

Oh wondrous steam'n wiener
couldn't shake you
or bounce you or trade you
in for a beaner
Yet unlike Fesston Bullvis
Prepuce Perry longed the night
told lies bout' his hot dog
Great, perspiring, glistening, greasy
meat tubes
cradled in an undeniable soft toasted
wonder.
'GOD ALMIGHTY,' he snort's

'CHICKEN FRANK'
cradled tenderly in an undeniable soft
toasted Wonder.
'GODALMAIGHTY,' he snorts, 'CHICKEN FRANKS!!!'"

Press reports when we have the attention span, no cash for the bar,
in detox, or are just bored silly alone in the rumpus room. Ten
dollar reading fee, per page (comes in handy),
We promise to read your poetry or at least have somebody read
it. (Money orders please) self-addressed/postage paid is
a very good idea (another good idea is to make those money orders
out to "cash") In closing the editor states.....

"The state of poetry in America is nearly invisible. As a rule poets
don't really like each other, read each other's stuff only to steal,
and in general are a pack of howling/sniveling jackals, endlessly
jealous bastards over anybody else's successes and gleeful about
the failures. We can think of no other group that has done more
to strangle and destroy honest, passionate, spontaneous prose and
poetry."

Spring 88

WELCOME TO THE PACIFIC RIM RACE WARS

Time for a little break in the action, there daily
routine cancer America, lift your head up to regard the
comfort Prozac laced citizen void lurching out of the
cars that ring with the bells of shopping center elevators.
Time to pick up that box of Cranberry dental floss for
your cat and curl his lips; feigning Lord God Elvis
spare tire hips. Peruse the menu, whistle appreciatively
smack the air while rubbing the sweaty palms of your
pudgy paws lusting a little snack platter of
mini-malls morphing into the Techno-Tropolis.

Setting: LAPD Grid MAP 6 reference: the Southwest
Subdivision of point intersect: 759B. Location Code:
Alpha/Omega Sector; Double Z V N, Mile post block 22.
(No defects)
Meanwhile, back in real time you can hear the ticking
sound in the curfew hushed air. Over the electric short
in the speakers, seconds are marching in an incendiary
single file.
Location and destination: Operation Angel Guard, the
LAPD master plan for the protection of the city of Los
Angeles in the event of a general break down of order
and massive civil unrest and destruction of public and
private property.

Prefer to hunker down in your fortified prosperity Pill-
Box and slumber bunker than to see the real thing live???
It's O.K. Coming soon in a recently reclaimed charred
battle field/neighborhood near you. Have another big
bag of Miro-hastabe, grease coated reality negating popcorn
knocking-your-block-off video center.
Remember make tonight a Martial Law night.

And if you act now, we will include exclusive vouchers
on a first come, first serve basis your looter-sized canister
of Official L.A.P.D. Pepper Gas. Be one of the first 100
lucky paranoid citizenoids and your bonus gift will be the
extended CD/Video recording of the Southern California's
State Police and National Guards HHHOOOOOTTTT
new collaboration entitled; "The Achy, Breaky Crowd Control
Dance." It's easy and fun. You thrill to watch actual footage
of real handsome young brutal Lucas-like-Storm Troopers
actually performing a run-through in the parking lots of
Dodger Stadium. In no time you'll be joining into the
excitement; Just repeat after me; Crossbow; Pulsate and Bump.
Crossbow, Pulsate and Bump. Everybody's talking about
those thrilling synchronized jet-black jack-boots that just keep
going and going and going and marching and marching goose
stepping like cute little pink bunny Nazis. You'll be awe
struck at the power-sticking aluminum batons glistening and
glinting in the pale grey-yellow smog like an other-world
illumination of the "Illuminati."

Remember you are the chosen. You live out in
Fort Suburbia, where it's property values.. Uber alles
in the new community order, at an electronic town
hall meeting you can near the minor league council-person
of your district sneer over a big plate of Bar-B-Q ribs,
"It's more police, stupid." As this hour's "FACTOID"
enlightens you that in the Pico-Union district of Los Angeles

called "Little Central America" there are over 147 people packed per square Acre!!" (Just a little footnote that population per square foot density is 4x's the density of New York City.)

Soon to be released on home-video, even before it occurs, It's the Pacific Rim Race Wars of the turn of the century. SHUDDER......as the assembled minority groups watch their hope and options diminish as they try and outbox each other for the three point play of 5 dollar an hour factory jobs. SHRUG.....as the new blood feuds of the year 2000 over the count and amount of T-cells replace gang warfare. IGNORE it all...as you tool coolly by in multi-colored fiber glass computerized high-impact Charioteer 99, the last word in apocalyptic luxury, complete with cellular phone/police access scanner units connected directly into CHiP's helmets, credit card terminal direct down load link to the friendly local convenient branch of your bank. Traffic jam, got you down, well just flip on the in dash 120 cable station system and watch that carnivorous New Anchor Creature provide the updates on the limited nuclear exchange in the middle East and latest stock market reports for Tokyo and Bonn. Brought to you by Reebok, because here on planet Reebok there are no rules. Your positive termination papers are being faxed. Sit back and enjoy this Xerox moment.

92-95

APRIL MORN

When the April morning turns into an envelope
and licks itself sealed back toward the twilight
then the first bolts of lightning flash like young
colts across the sky.
Downpour the early morn in thunder roar
again in this year's voice, turning back to the
page where the dark rumble left off.
The end of the world will come in summer.
Fall would be of course a trifle dramatic.
An all-inclusive world wide production number
with millions of extras.
The veneer of civilization will be shorn off the packaging
crate of our inherent savagery like a Black and Decker
Saber Tooth 2000 circular saw slicing six inch plywood in
a black steady line.
The top will drop off rather quickly.
And from deep inside will come out all those
who were locked in the prisons. Just or unjust.
The new thunder will walk.
Back into a culture that never let them get to anything.
There will be old scores to settle.
Those who were never good enough, beautiful or lucky,
the poor, the white trash, the butts of your jokes;
the plain, the simple, all those who simply could not
fit into this virtual emerging hyper/stupor-reality. In this
time when the illusion is the dominant wisdom. With so few,
so much power contriving attractive lies into desire for the
many, it's not a matter of don't touch that dial anymore,

it's I'll zap your ass into the weather channel so fast that
no one will ever remember your last word. Unless, of course,
it was an ice commercial where all were frozen in youth to
empty bottles of manipulation with cheap, slick catchy labels.

When the fiber optic looking glass of vanity blinks
out and our model H-O railroad town must join hands with all
the others in the roaring darkness. We may then perhaps
get a glimpse of the howling hoax that has been perpetrated.

So it may not be a matter of the end of the world.
Maybe just the end of the conveniently ignorable one.

The start of the new season. When the new thunder
will walk. Past the Camera whore backlit on the beach
in that certain light and in a semi-Gregorian chant we
hear rising from the shell of a freshly looted Bob Evans,
"You know I've been Mcliving this Mclife so long that
I don't know what I'm Mcfucking doing anymore."

The pace of rapid change of the world will at last
catch up with itself. And then it will catch up to you.

4/94

BELLINGHAM REMEMBERED

(For M.S.B.)

It was somewhere back along
those dark long streets
where you have someone to call back to you.
Where the lights in the Harbor at midnight
shimmered like smoldering embers
left in a huge black wet ashtray.

Her smile clean, bright in the wind
on the hilltop on a Sunday
relieved that she wasn't pregnant,
while the freights blue and white
left the yards below.

All the mornings and the midnights
twist in the rustle of the wind from
another time and coastline past.
My fingers remember the touch of mystery
in your street light silhouette;
an empty sidewalk, your window up
on the second floor darkened and
then the long bicycle ride home.

Where sweet faces sit still with their
longings adrift in the harbor while
a cold room is warmed by an ancient
space heater from Buffalo that grins bright
that orange in the dark blue dawn.

So where were you?

Somewhere along those dark long streets
you have someone to call back to you
the lights down below in the harbor
that looked like smoldering embers
in a huge black ashtray.

Her smile in the clean bright wind
of the morning after on the hilltop
Sunday relieved because she wasn't
pregnant while the freights
blue and white
leave the yards below

                                        79,94

YEAR END

What fades in this so quickly
the moment of softness
a succession of muted lights
winking from brutal everyday corners
into the uncertain blackness of the future.
Tell me different, then
show me the hope that eludes
that promise of reconciliation
the purpose for these days that provides
vibrance and glory.
The flip of the pages to a good passage
chapter and verse.
The voice that invites
the beckoning eyes that call you
by name. Your way illuminated
by light that shows a path
between the awful dead ends of dull routine.

Where is my seat?
My tasks? My charges?
Who looks for me?
How will I recognize them?

Now is the time.
Now can only be the time.
The time for release.

12/94

SONG OF APRIL

Verkhovyna
Here her face seldom lights
up on her own;
Still certain pictures stick
Adverted gaze quick
No sharing that glance shot in chilly
open light.
Verkhovya.

Outside the Madison Square at a quarter to spare.
Blur breath Amtrak ticketed back to Buffalo.
Early Sunday sidewalking madman weaving tight figure 8's.
Yelling, singing at the top of his lungs from a block and
a half away..... "Hut ut ooo Great Balls of Fire."
"Hut ut oo Goodness Gracious."
"Ut ut oo o me oh my."
"Gonna try with all of my might."

Just once more given the ride
Across the dream face, with a close friend at an elbow
We stood in the parking lot in Queens at Sunset
Waiting for a night under the Mercury arc vapors.

Verkhovya.

In a world past promise
to weld unto your actions
so that we could all get to the second reel (at last)

on the projectionist schedule.

He's going to have to re-thread another can of film
to fly open past the white burning carbon rods.

Illumination?
Sure. But first beyond contrived, convoluted tragic self
consciousness toxic society choking on what has been
degenerated into chemical things; New Mutants for an old
dance. Hordes of productivity managers coolly eyeing your
plate of wings, charting your beer intake like pitching the
next day in the board room employee behavior molding and
modification center. Thinking....one finger means: Educable
Two fingers: Terminate. Three Fingers: Screwball
Four Fingers: Pitch around him.

Personal Habits? The inside of his car smells of beer and
french fries sealed hermetically since 1977 split-fingered
in your face in a paranoid diatribe.

Verkhovyna
Have another go at all the stew, there you fucking panel
of experts. Let's go and do jingoism together some afternoon soon.
Face full of time, you yawn and page through the illusionary
sustained at a cost of millions.

Thinking "I can afford....not to give a rat's ass to a jackass
or....maybe if you're poor enough to have the privilege of
the honor to support and finance the collapse of what's left
of the old whore Camelot, remember when you used to like
        to sing
and dance a lot?
Verahovyna.
Seems like we just consumed and forgot a lot.

This time of season, when the song of April is on

the promise.
The glare is hard off the busy blank faced storefront
bullying products and services rendered for common tender,
Here sing. Hear blow a suspended moment
from a tarnished, brass, muted trumpet.
Supper smells fill the coming sliding shadows
of dusk. Here where clear water seconds pour off in a
Fellahin bucket. Twilight struck cymbals shimmer in long
relief. I just stopped in here to duck it.
A predictable routine. Two days in the stiff saddle of
remote control tag and grey long cable afternoons,
Just pushing the damned button over and over,
giving anything about fifteen seconds.
Cultural amnesia in the concept of no longer understanding
what the word, "contradiction" means. Fruit and Fiber rapist
(and we lost dat darsh gone super bowl by....... that much.)
Same old thing, I fix the ladder on your fire truck
and you just walk away.
Verkhovya.

In the morning, resurrection's come
in blindness to everyone
open go all the eyes
taken for granted miracles
rain or shine
yours or mine.
Our snug fragile mounds of ease

Leaving Kathy Lee with Regis
and her hair to tease.
Common neighbor unit-tombs of complicity, complacency and
redundancy.
A now one final soliloquy; Cross Horatio, Hamlet and the
drunk from the face on the bar room floor doing a variation
on, "Alas, Poor Yorick", now add Dice Clay wanna be hips
pointed, extended Marlboro, doing Greek tragedy, with

a Shakespearian Brooklynese in Italian,

"Adesso parliano, a , quattr'occlui."

1991

SUPPER TIME

In the first chill of any dusk
the gathering in November
put vermilion in blue blankets
and put your dreams to bed.

When the chilly air smells like a menu
but you're being sent to your room without any supper.

Tonight's Special is vapor.

There is this fresh watercolor gone slightly stiff
to walk out into
one sidewalk year at a time.
Just waiting for your everyday heel and toe
to provide demarcation, passage and impression.

Here is the supper time on earth
where all is ordered and consumed flesh.

It comes in by the mouthful
or the plateful
The carlot; the hopper; the carousal caress.
Here all that has been grown
has been harvested if in season
seeds did flourish.

Inside the breath is of forced air
that rustles invisible fingers
running across the
fine hairs on the back of your neck
till there is this brush back
and your container rots off
and you're never hungry again.

Summer 92

SLAPPING THE ID

Stay up late
make a good bid
you're an awful big boy
to still be
slapping your id.

I know what you said.
I heard what you did.
You had better start thinking
in terms of a lid.

So go ahead you
stay up late
and put in a bid
but remember you're an awful big boy
to still be
slapping the id.

91

UNTITLED

Somber October
tells leaves
time to dress
in the vivid cloak of death.

Don't be fooled by this
warm afternoon.
You know how this will end up.
You've seen this all before.
The yellow jackets are out
crawling on the sidewalk.
They have their marching orders.

October sat up and said,
"Get your boots and wet suit;
we have just enough time and
precisely the right amount of lead.
Your season ends swiftly.
Fall comes in swinging sneakers
and hanging long laces.
The music starts
Fall ties the laces
on its shoes around
our necks
and asks, "Anybody here wanna dance?"

PURPOSE

In the early afternoon
she paused in the shimmer light of fresh March
where hung the potted green plants
and in the shafts of sunlight
the cheeks of her ass
protruded and hung like two twin
cherry gum drops.
(Didn't that sugar sparkle too?)
To him it looked like a cookie
jar, that he was told he never could
touch, no matter how good a boy he had been.
"Too bad," he thought, "that's about it."

Winter 87

OUTTA TOWN

Your face won't be there tonight.
The sound and the picture will,
but you'll be elsewhere;
maybe on a train or a bus
on your way home, on the turnpike
coming back from the mall.
Time will be just something else
that passed. A voice left hanging
in the air elsewhere.
Gentle cheekbones dark burrows for the
lost soft brown eyes that brim
bar sweat and whispers at dawn,
in that place, where your face
won't be tonight.

91

BIG SILENCE

Every afternoon he walks across the lawn
and hangs unwanted papers in shrink wrap
on the door knob.
On the pages are used car sales; brand new
deals on roto tillers and SWF 22 crestfallen
dark eyed question mark looking for a certain
position with a older professional pervert,
non-smoker, non-drinker, non-premature ejaculating
sugar daddy conveniently located
in a nearby shopping center.

It makes you look twice
but now Shhhhh.
His favorite beer commercial is on.

Dribble a La Carte.
Or was that K-Mart,
where subject to availability
you could own
the entire 12 step program,
"How to live with an Elad."

So how many faces will it take him tonight?
What version is this?
Hoist up the pages
and spill your wrist's action
in lines that glare at the apparition
between the partition

with the cardboard snotty looks.
So, we were dismissed
told not to worry, he'll be back with more words of
wisdom from Joe-Joe the dog faced boy.
So here's the rabbit in black face pleading,
"now don't you throw me in that briar patch."

I'll just radio for back up
and till it comes
watch the clock on the wall
all hands and boneyard white
full of cold marble
just read the name
and the time in
and the time out.
Perhaps read the small inscription,
I've seen better guys than you
dead twenty years already in
country and western songs.

91-93

OH BRIGHT BEERY MIRAGE

The foot falls came in cans up and down the neighbor's
stairs. Can after can of foot falls fan while the
neighbors stare in the good seats just over to the left.
We still preferred the super 8 or was that the figure 8?
So what's begging a solution to that damn grainy resolution
the unresolved plot conflict, the lack of character
development and a forgettable series of mundane settings
in which little ever happened except some uptight dog down
the block had decided that it was his big night to bark.

In the other room images of the last nine decades
were flipped around like a bored wife at the remote control
Shit/more products/Swaggart swimming in tears/shit/
more products/a parade of cheap whores who told him they
won't even let the kids watch/ 1950 Wesson oil/ 1963 dead
widows of murdered presidents living a hideous tragedy
to the grave alone wondering why the skillet got that
hot that quick.

Addressing the congregation of bored shadows he asked
should I call 911 or yell "pull" or don't you have
a preference?

After all since the last time we waltzed each other
around by the shirt collars at four A.M. I'm still picking
up match wood in the front yard. And don't tell me again

how handy it's all gonna come in someday.

Without so much as a plot or even needle neck pliers
he took turns leading either them or himself around by
the nose, still intent on getting or providing one
good laughable punch line or defensive explanation that
digressed to our right bold faced lying alibis that hadn't
worked ten years ago, but nobody in the room was around then,
so why not give them another whirl.

If not, it was time enough to say goodbye I guess you
knew me when, knew me where, knew enough to see
        through me
then and into the yard next door after the visiting gluttonous
dignitaries had eaten and puked; eaten and puked once more
their way through the 11th hour promises of justice and
a herd of upper lip-less Doug Llewelyn's sneering in superior
haughty tones about not taking the law in your own hands.

But let's not overreact. Truth was they looked you up
and down painfully polite and precisely ambivalent with a
steely eyed blank eye expression that suggested, "your
intestines could drop out of your asshole right now like
sweet polish sausages and I'd never even suggest home made
wine mustards."

And then, old friend it's "Bon Appetite."

So it's hail, hail, the gang's all here.
Anybody got a quarter, gotta make a phone call and
dime the whole bunch into the local authorities for
cash prizes and future considerations.
Remember if you know at least what you don't want
prepare a nice itemized list.
It'll save time and dreams.

And if you're all out of imagination
All out of cable channels
All out of VCR's
All out of CD's
All out of fashion sense
Just take a station break and heave a long, slow sigh
BUT....
Don't screw around with the illusion of your freedom
better NOT take the lid off that selfish sneering veneer.
The me-ism marked down from I-ism till it all sort of
degenerated into I don't have any idea-ism and I don't
give a shit-ism anymore.

So next morning, they'll all just show up at your door
stinking of butts, suds and attitude, holding their heads
and mewing some whining bullshit about being little kittens
that have lost their mittens and are afraid now that they just
aren't going to get any pie.
You can stand there, thumbs in the loop holes of your
pants swinging on the balls of your heels and tell them
to go fry some ice, try and get it brown, if not wrap it
in some tin foil and stick it in the microwave.
Then you can slam the door like gallows plywood
gaping hole in a nightmare where your mouth snaps open
like a side entrance used only in cause of fire and other
emergencies and yell at the top of your lungs, "Thank you
and goodnight."

88/94

ROSES FOR THORNS

I grew worried I wasn't a poet anymore.
So I fasted and prayed. Prayed and fasted.
I went to the cable wilderness of TBS.. and CNN
and lived on meat and water for thirty days and
thirty nights. Nothing changed.
The town fathers adorned in jackboots stomped the night
into dawn on the floor above. The drinking and laughter
flowed like a torrent of sludge, townie salmon swimming
upstream toward middle age. Stunned and hung-over,
they were slow to fade.
   Yet soon the dreams began again
I was back in July afternoons, when the beach was still there.
Now with a son, at last come out from behind the clouds,
to walk down the shoreline, about two and a half feet tall,
to reach up and grasp my hand.
   July still the fullest of dresses/offshore
breeze that rustles her hem making quick work of the memory
of all that sallow water, wanting badly a bridge to be under,
a river to be down and past, at last.
I think the tide has worn me down a bit.
I think the tide has worn away all the poems
along with the sand grains, pebbles, once stones, once rocks,
once boulders, once a continental drift, just going along for
the ride with an ice age.
I was worried about the present day geology of poetry,
in terms of, what have we been ground down to, so far?
I guessed I should ask? But who?
I looked at the faces. They didn't seem likely choices.

In fact, I discovered that there wasn't anyone to ask.
All they wanted were the negatives: so...here they are:
This pen stinks. The typewriter is nothing more than a
glorified vibrator with prostate problems.
This damn thing is fat, bored, judgmental, defensive,
a cable-ready self-assured bore. Its perspective is unwilling
to change, learn, or be inspired. And worse yet, your attention
is demanded. Your reward?
The payoff will be in a blurry, goose stepping, product march
promising fulfillment and smugness.
Maybe an occasional blow-job or maybe a drug czar or two.
What I worried about most was told to me this morning.
No more poets, no way, said the Gumbo on Today, just
Willard with his head in the microwave, door snug on his neck,
with the roast beef setting on the dial. You've got just enough
time to go to the kitchen, make a quick sandwich, and make it
back in front the T.V. to hear Jean-Luc Picard say,
    "ENGAGE" for the next twenty years.
  So you can see my deep concern over this matter.
The matter of all the missing poetry. All the missing poems.
All the poets missing poetry. Maybe I was missing anyone who
understands all this or gives a good beaker of pissed off lab
workers trying to determine whether that's Sudafed or Ecstasy
in your plastic Dixie cup of wee-wee, all for 7.35 a hour.
"It's clearly a matter of upbringing," drawls the fatman with the
Hop-Along-Cassidy hat, round wire glasses and the walrus
        mustache,
in between the heaping mouthfuls of "it's the right thing to do"
gruel.
  "If you were raised on Pollock, Parker and Brautigan in the lobby
of 1938 Deco-Desperado movie theaters, had a popcorn
problem as a youth, attended Catholic Schools, were told
you couldn't join the boy scouts or little league,
because your old man
didn't believe in communist organizations.

If you knew teenage junkies,
anti-intellectual snobs, fell in love with the local ice-princess
and felt the wrath and fish eye of just plain ole fashion
common hating folks, took those LSD holidays with Billie and
cultivated the world view that
all indications and omens in the sky
(along with the considered opinion of speed freak gutter
Nostradamus) told you it should have been all over by now!!
IN A MUSHROOM MINUTE,
IN A HYDROGEN HEARTBEAT.
ALL RIGHT ALREADY!!!!
What we really need is Yogi Berra to get in here
shove Willard's fat ass out of the way and stick his fuckin
head in the microwave and say, "HEY IT'S OVER"!!!!!!!

But what's THIS supposed to be then?????????
Your plastic handcuffs to the stars?
Please stand by.
We are standing by.
Waiting for them to fix.
Please fix.
We don't understand any of all this.
Please fix it.
And you know what?
They are working on it.
Still the world spins on year after year.
They don't have any control over that yet.
It spins. We go along for the ride.
Taking, taking, taking.
Consuming everything, producing nothing but garbage.

Putting nothing back in.
While this place gets smaller, meaner,
a paler shade of humorless grey tinted smoke windows
full of blank stares in the January parking lot of Zayres.

And now all this despair has seeped into here.
And on top of that, you don't run across any poets to ask
about all this anymore. Any successful one, will tell you to
speak to his accountant and pick up his latest C.D. while he
bends over in the me-mirror going...."Hey dude.... my close
friends... they'll humor me, with comfort and support.
Like "We always knew you were full of shit and
NOW you have the nerve to start to whine
about losing the way or you can't find any
poets, listen why don't you call up
American Gladiators and see if
they wanna start an English Lit. hit-squad for aging men boys
enamored with their own twisted trite dreary sentiments???
There's a new world a coming.
There pal, and with your present
attitude in tow, you and the ozone layer got something in
common. While that Sage, good old Snagglepuss in the corner
    of
the bar is shaking his head saying...
"WE TOLD YOU YEARS AGO,
THAT ALL THAT POETRY JAZZ WAS NOWHERE!!!!"

O.K. There. You can have that way. All yours. You win.
You're right. All this is nowhere. So bigshot here's the payoff.
I'll tell you about the dream that came to me in some twilight.
Dawn. It was all about roses.
Here's some roses for your thorns.
In any room, where we are all in this, the big-house earth.
You should be so blessed to dream the fabric of July.
Who dreams? Those that need to.
Those who need to give each other
another brilliant summer shoreline to stroll on.
To have the need to think all day poems with impossible
clusters of tiger lilies daring to bloom out of season.
To need to explain to your son, why the gulls lust french fries

yellow greasy delicious cold, even coated with grit.
Who will tell us, who will remind them, what the world was
like just a moment ago, if we do not make the effort?

    Yes..my fire is burning. Yes. The ashes are hot.
Yes. You need to keep your powder dry and cool.
Especially if you're storing them in the same room
Yes. You need to transcend a bitter uptight techno-society of
power men squares and the latest thing in inquisitional Nazis.
To put them off. To put them on. To assure them of their
    victory.

To beam at them and say,
"We will throw roses at your thorns."
For when the cement curtains in the dusk are falling
you must hear the concrete sunrise calling
in a voice gone raspy; with a touch of fingers
barely grazing the fine hairs of the forearm at dawn.

To awaken and remember, from this our only dream.
So we will have a song to sing for each other:
an embrace to offer
a Poem to tell.

                                      October 90

THE INTERVIEW

They sat on the far corners of the table with the appearance of a bland, bored tribunal of a modern workplace tribute to the mundane having a small degree of power.

The position that they were reviewing the applicants for was a tedious, complicated over-blown baby sitting job for a bunch of Federal Grants that they were in part drawing a portion of their salaries from. The job duties were to be split between a knack for simplistic attention to paperwork and ability to solve your own problems on your own time. No explanations. No guide lines. No encouragement. Just accountability.

The candidate understood and had experience with this type of situation before. Basically, what it boiled down to was: here are your tools (a fire axe) and there your job site (Limbo) now go build something. Don't bother us with questions, requests for guidance or support. Just get to work. We'll let you know what's wrong with it when we feel like it. We'll drop by for inspection someday when you've built something and tell you why it stinks and what's wrong with it. Any back talk. You're fired. Any questions. You're fired. Any displays of intelligence, creativity, or backbone. You're fired.

He walked in the room to sit across from them. They exchanged superficial, trite, saccharine pleasantries.

It started off well enough. The one at the far end who evidently supported him read some nice thing that his references had told her. The middle one looked bored and tired. There was a yawn or two stifled. The process lurched along. It was uneventful. Then the fat one squatting at the other end of the table went to work.

Eyeing him like he was certainly an impostor, at the very least an inappropriate waste of her time, she hissed out an icy appraisal.

"Well, you haven't ever held a full time job..have you?

She held in her two Twinkie fingers his resume at a distance like it was a feces splattered forged document. Her air of general scepticism was only usurped by her obvious disgust.

She arched her left eyebrow and made a face like she needed immediate bowel movement and pursing the liver lips spat out.

"Your work history. . . . is rather. . . . spotty. . . . now isn't it?"

He thought, "Yeah a lot like that adult diaper you squeeze into every morning."

He wasn't going to say anything like that yet. Best he could do was mumble out some explanation about budget cuts, temporary assignments, shifting work base, the usual crap..

She wasn't buying any of it. She was already looking at the next applicant's resume. The other members of the tribunal were beginning to shift uncomfortably in their seats.

It was obvious who was in charge here.

She continued, "There seems to be a gap here between 1986 and 1987. What were you doing at that time?

He let out a long sigh. He would give conventional civility one more try.

"Well that must be a typo. Look, the information on my "Vita" isn't merely the whole picture to consider it's just a delineated map of sorts, providing a general written outline of dates and their corresponding positions."

"Your what?" she said with a sardonic incredibility. "My Vita," he replied, "it's a Latin word for life."

"O I see," she bubbled like trapped swamp gas escaping several layers of rancid sludge. She paused for effect and continued with a mocking serious gravely elongated phrasing, "that means I hold your "life" in my hands". Then she smiled triumphantly as if she had just mainlined a hypo of fudge and grease into her veins.

You could cut the silence in the room with a cheese slicer.

The tension was growing like swelling and heaving tubes of bologna being inflated from within, threatening to explode.

Enough. The candidate cut loose.

"You know, it's not that I mind going through this processing, so much. Even though it's a bit like having people off the street look up your asshole. It's the accompanying small change power trips that the protoplasm-challenged wobble butt sour-pussed types put you through."

"Sure I need this fuckin job. Sure I can do it. You know that. And if you decide something different fine. Let's just leave it at that and quit trying to floss my meatus. And as for you," he turned toward her face which was now frozen in mid-stupor like a block of beef tripe carved into somewhat human features stuffed into a seventy buck Dacron-Polyester flower print one size fits all summer dress from Wal-Mart.

"It's what you represent that gets to me. The decisions you make help shape the world a little more into a reflection of yourself. And evidently there isn't much room in the mirror for anyone else's way of living or thinking. The only thing narrow about you there, pie-hole, are your thoughts. It would appear that you look at the small hold you have on the corner of the world like it was your own personal refrigerator and nobody, but nobody is getting within whiffing distance of that handle on the door. Believe it or not, I've been in your shoes. I know what they smell like, where they have or have not been. You are the concentrated ugliness of a repressive hateful system, that has way too much authority and power and way too little vision, compassion or vibrance. Your small minded bitterness and adolescent revenge minded world view makes me want to puke.

"It is my summation that the only satisfaction, purpose and orgasm in your life you achieve is your ability to say no to people that you feel threatened by, because of their nerve to be different from you. This isn't an interview. It's a minor league career inquisitional mini-camp for co-dependent professional cowards devoted to maintaining a stringent level of mediocrity in their chosen field."

The Tribunal sat stunned.

All except her. She slowly released a greasy, craggy grin while tilting her head slightly on an angle and calmly spoke,

"Well... that is very interesting and where would you like to be in five years?

9/94

NAME THAT SMELL

(For D.L.)

I have a writer friend whom I've known for about twenty years. Our friendship has had many levels.

We have seen each other in a variety of shapes, forms and fortunes. I was his student once. The biggest gift he ever imparted was the idea that expression was free. Everyone could express themselves to some degree. All experiences were valid and valuable. You could dream and endeavor to be published, but that was not the deciding factor of an individual's success in the love of an art form. It was a philosophy that was oddly juxtaposed with the current wisdom defining creative expression. The implication was you could not judge your own work, everything hinged on what those who had position or power defined as "good."

"Good" meant "marketable" and that meant that someone who could give a crap about your "artistic" message or format could make money off of your "talent." Of course, it seemed just about anyone who worked in the arts would fork over their soul to the first corporate sponsor with a fist full of cash. This was to be expected. The line of would be musicians, actors, writers, poets, artists, and dancers perpetually stretched out the door, down the street, and around the corner.

The dance of the wanna-be's, one trick ponies and never were has been hacks was a conga line to obscurity. The tune was "FAME, I'm gonna live forever."

Let's get this straight right now, once and for all. This is not the theme song for self-indulgent cynic to qualify lack of perspective or dramatic vehicle. It's a short tale about the new price on every day expression. My writer friend and I had just given a poetry reading in a small college town in the next state over. It had been a great night. For once it was my friend that offended somebody with his work and not me. I was put in the unlikely position of peace maker and ruffled feather smoother. I told the pissed off party to relax, that my friend was not the intentionally vicious type, I on the other hand was the one who usually put my foot either in it or my mouth. The guy bought it and all was well. My friend and I rolled back into town with semi-thick wads of one dollar bills to bank roll our beers. We had gotten a take of the door at the reading.

We were in very good moods. It was just after midnight. We walked into the bar, ordered up and grinned at each other rather pleased with the whole evening. The bar was nearly empty. The owner sat down by himself near the window. He looked a little low. He was a friend of ours, we went down to cheer him up. It turned out he was a little depressed over the impending death of live local amateur bands in the bars of the small college town. We asked him to explain.

"Well, he said, "it seems that in order to feature any live musical acts, regardless if they play original or cover songs, I've got to fork over a considerable fee to cover their dues to this so-called professional musicians union. I could never cover it at the door with an admission charge and pay the band anything. In fact I would lose money even with well known regional acts, they can't even play for free." What shit we agreed. It really did stink. The owner of the bar invited us down stairs to look at the official information he had. We followed him down to the office. We watched him shift through piles of papers looking for it. He was having trouble finding it. I looked around the walls of the office. They were covered with twenty years of past advertisements for hundreds of little college and local bands. It had been their big gigs. It had been the time of their lives. It was all over now. It was like someone had invented a variation on the protection racket to regulate small town musical expression. The owner swore and finally gave up. He couldn't find the article he was looking for. We all went back up stairs to the bar.

It was a little more crowded. The first thing I noticed was this horrible smell. It permeated the barroom. My friend and I walked down to the other end of the bar. The smell was stronger there. I looked at my pal and said, "what the fuck is going on?" "WHAT THE HELL IS THAT SMELL???"

We looked down the bar. I watched the face of this beautiful woman twitch and begin to melt. The sour pungent odor of rotted fish/eggs/feces/feet/cheese/sulfur clorox hung so thick in the air you couldn't cut it with a Chain Saw. I gagged. My pal looked at me helplessly. Then I spotted the source. At the bar, calmly ordering a fresh beer stood this guy with white painters pants on. Only they weren't quite white anymore. Unbelievably down both sides of the insides of his trousers, there was this dark brown river of stain that extended from crotch to ankles. That son of a bitch was nonchalantly standing at the bar holding up two bucks to the bartender fudged from stem to stern. I had an ugly vision of pools in his shoes.

He had a beatific innocent blankness on his face. "O my God," I gasped. My friend and I ran to the back of the bar and found the owner in the kitchen. I said in a poker faced deadpan, "Hey Bud, I think somebody up in the front of the bar needs a hand." The owner looked puzzled. "Hey. What the hell is that?" asked the cook who had appeared holding his nose.

"You don't want to know, for Christ sake open that door here." He did. And we all gratefully drank in the clear cold fresh night air. I tried to take a swig of my beer. The smell was stuck in the bottle. I whipped it at the dumpster. I turned my back to the barroom. It was after all an embarrassing situation for all concerned. I was just glad I didn't have to deal with that guy up front in the bar. Man, was I wrong. About fifteen minutes passed and the bar owner came back to where we were standing.

He held out in his hand two business cards, they were brown smudged and they stank. I recoiled in horror.

"What the hell are those?"

The owner shook his head and said, "Business cards from the representative of ASCAP He wants you and Dave to give him a call."

"Who the hell is that?"

"The guy from the organization I was telling you about that monitors local artist expression."

"What the hell does he want?"

"He wants to tell you about the new surcharge on the poetry readings you guys do."

"I can't believe it"

"Believe it, pal." the bar owner said.

I turned to look up the barroom. It had cleared out again. The bartender was walking up and down spraying some evergreen scented Lysol all around.

My friend asked, "Hey what about that guy with the load in his pants, what was his story."

The bar owner looked at both of us like we were as slow as sludge.

"You stupid asses, have you been listening to anything I've been saying.... WHO THE HELL DO YOU THINK I'VE BEEN TELLING YOU ABOUT!!!!!

Winter 95

DREAM 27

I was sitting on a bench in a darkened park.

The emptiness was ringing in my ears. I looked to the left and then to the right, there was not a sound to be found. Everything looked brittle and black. Any lights seemed garish and shone thinly like razor slits in the facades of the town's store fronts. I at once became aware of the fact I was not by myself. I turned my head to look over my shoulder and she was sitting there on another bench. She had an odd slight expression of tender recognition on her face. I said to her, "I thought I was alone." She replied, "You don't know what loneliness is until you've met Nancy." I knew what kind of dream this was. I got up and walked over to where she was sitting and she stood up. I stood before her and when we embraced I was startled by the feeling of her bulky jacket and the warmth of her light frame pressing upon mine. Her arms circled upon my shoulders. Our faces inches apart. Her breath on my face was honeyed. I was astounded. I stepped back. And she tilted her head and her eyes glistened while her lips parted slightly. Then she vanished into thin air.

Winter 94

THE EMPIRE'S CASH REGISTER STRIKES BACK

Welcome to a nation of suspects reduced for quick clearance marked down to citizenoids of the PLANET HOLLYWOOD. Home for a global theme park called McWORLD.

Spare me the snotty looks and just dive back into the infotainment of your telesector. Here in McWORLD empowerment lies in the choice of toppings on the franchised nourishment of the market moment place. Shiver in seductive delight to McWorld's enticing blend of commerce, manipulated desire and vicarious satisfaction.

Here comes the endless parade of washed out emaciated pouting waifs strutting down the mandatory fashion runway.

See them sashay in your future with brutally handsome dark men brimming with cruelty and scorn for all not as young and stunning as they.

All you can do is buy a ticket and watch:
Watch: without responsibility
Watch: without engagement
Watch: without consequences.

Sieg heil, Vox populi !
Sieg heil. Vox Populi !

Here where McWorld's Affairs of State are reported via the 24 hr Sports channel called "Smart Ass Center"
Complete with rapping commentators honing there personal

demeanor and delivery style of Benito Mussolini.
Welcome to the cartooning of reality.
The subtle grace and charm of Ren and Stimpy.
Empirical Beavis. The ever articulate Butt-Head.
And the best part? And the best part?
If the acceleration in the rate of appetite and tolerance
for contrived, boorish vulgarity continues to increase at
the present exponential rate guess the next faces of which
blatant Morons will be carved on Mount Rushmore to greet
the new century?

Empty V Empty V I want my Empty V.
The Newsweek in Newspeak via Wal-Mart Think.

Once upon a time in the 19th Century the great newborn
corporate monopolies dealt in oil, steel, coal and
railroads. Those muscles of the modern industrial body
have been replaced by control of images, pictures,
information, ideas battling
for dominance of the mind of McWorld's soul.
Now in McWorld, Rockefeller "morphs" Snoop doggy dog style
into Bill Gates. Carnegie into Spielberg. Vanderbilt into Oprah.
Then Michael Jackson at last settles that whole business of
"the chicken and the egg question" with new philosophic inquiry:
"Is he a boy or a man?"
The resounding answer, who cares? He's a product.

We are the consumers.
The nature of this commodity not to your liking?
Don't worry McWorld can get it for you "wholesale."

Did you ever get the feeling we are all waiting for something?
As we sit in the room and watch the news without the sound on
like it was a silent movie, but Buster Keaton will not appear
in a sad sullen face to peer out at us uncomprehending.

Are we waiting for that rogue, errant mile wide asteroid to settle this hash on the planet Reebok, Planet Hollywood, for the planet formerly known as earth.
Maybe it's time for a little EVOLUTIONARY housecleaning and fix this docudrama and provide an eternity of close captioning for the post-modern impaired.
(Kinda like the X-files meets Dr. Quinn in the middle of decade of nuclear winter)

   I used believe, fear, hope that McWorld would never have gotten this far. Nuclear war, environmental collapse, social upheaval would have claimed all this long ago. Maybe God would come back. Or send shiny aliens to separate the wheat from the chaff. But no.

What we are waiting for in McWorld is the ultimate product.
Something like: An athletic shoe equipped
with a fast food nutrition patch fastened to the coolest sunglasses
that inject coca-cola directly into the veins of the inner ear
while projecting the latest Empty-V video directly into the retina.
And of course the all new Mandatory
McWorld Declaration of Product Interdependence will repeat every 15 minutes and please won't you rise and repeat with me:

          WHEN IN THE COURSE OF CORPORATE EVENTS, IT BECOMES
PROFITABLE FOR FACELESS MULTI-NATIONAL POWER BASES TO DEFINE
AND PROVIDE ALL LIFE CHOICES, IDENTITY, DREAMS AND CONSUMPTION
FOR A NATION OF SUSPECTS WHO DON'T REALLY KNOW ANY BETTER AND DESERVE TO BE TREATED LIKE THE IGNORANT SHEEP THEY ARE. IT IS TRULY RIGHTEOUS AND JUST FOR AUTHORITARIAN CEO'S TO SUSTAIN THE MAINTENANCE OF POWER AND DOMINANCE BY ANY MEASURES FOR THE

JUSTIFICATION OF THE MEANS OF INFINITE GREED
AND LUST FOR PROFIT EQUALS THE ENDS
OF THE COMPLETE REDEFINITION OF GOD,
MANKIND, NATURE AND ALL LAWS OF ETHICS
GOVERNING OF HUMAN BEHAVIOR.
THE NEW McWORLD ORDER
HOLDS THESE TRUTHS TO BE
MANDATORY THAT ALL HUMAN BEINGS
ARE MERELY CONSUMERS, AND DULL
WITTED ONES AT THAT. ALL CONCEPTS OF A CREATOR
ENDOWING ANYONE WITH CERTAIN UNALIENABLE
RIGHTS WILL BE ERADICATED BY THE
IMAGINEERING DEPARTMENT OF McWorld
RESPONSIBLE FOR REDEFINING REALITY. THE NEW
UNALIENABLE RIGHTS OR WAS THAT NON-TRANSFER
ABLE OR GOOD WITH ANY OTHER OFFER OR COUPON
WILL BE THAT IN THE REALM OF McWORLD UNTIL
FURTHER NOTICE THE CONCEPT OF LIFE, LIBERTY
AND THE PURSUIT OF HAPPINESS
WILL BE REPLACED AS McWORLD
RENAMES THE UNITED STATES OF AMERICA AS MARKET
LAND. WHERE EVERYTHING, EVERYONE, EVERY
EMOTION, EVERY LOYALTY IS FOR SALE AND SOMEONE
ELSE ALWAYS IS RESPONSIBLE AND THERE ARE NO
COMMON GOODS OR PUBLIC INTERESTS AND WHERE
EVERYONE IS EQUAL AS LONG AS THEY CAN
AFFORD THE PRICE OF ADMISSION AND ARE CONTENT
TO WATCH AND CONSUME.
AMEN.

2/97

RAWMAN IN THE YARD

(For C.M.)

Your eyes roll back and the lids peel open.
Flutter upon the half-light of almost dawn.
RAWMAN doesn't dream anymore.
But he sure as hell can remember.

This was RAWMAN's yard. His holding area for the night.
And he's going to be very anxious for the first light.
All vision, all movement, all the rules
are different in this yard.

He is once again a very small child,
remembering the vast universe of his backyard.
They told you the rules. They were big.
So large, so tall, so important.
You can hear them telling you that there are certain
places in the yard for you to stay away from.
A nest of Yellow Jackets, a bramble of brown thorns,
a heap of glass shards, the uncertain ground of a cesspool.
The sun is out. It's hot and July. There's no shade.
You've been told to, "go outside and play."

RAWMAN spent all last night in the yard.
Was it sleep? It wasn't a nightmare
It was something far worse.
You were back in that yard with a new twist.

You felt just as small as you did the first time,
but now there was no voice to warn you where not
to step. This yard is different.
This is the yard of memory, elapsed years, action,
consequence and incident. This yard is truly as large or
as small as you have created it.
It contains every single thing you have ever done,
thought, felt or seen.

You're not dreaming RAWMAN, you're remembering.
What was it you did?
Or was that...what...you didn't do?
Knock around here for awhile.
Let's have the past take a good look at you.
And the darkest corner of the yard now is
that expanse towards the far end marked, "future."
It's a bad thing. You can see a kind of needle face.
The features are twisted into the shape of a head sized
funnel point. It pokes and pokes and swirls in a
menacing, snarling, snapping twirl. It was like they took
her features and made them out of a black and white ice
cream and let them melt and
whipped them into a pinwheel smear.
It turns and snarls and hisses at you, "ZZZZZzzzzzziiissssss
ssssssssssssshizz,....how would you like me to punctuate you?"
And now you're screaming, aren't you?
Not dreaming.
You're remembering
the face of that needle nosed smoke thing
You're remembering
your way around the yard.
Where you lost your heart, your ears, your eyes,
and they stole your dreams.

Now you're on the couch

with just enough hint of light in the sky
to suggest dawn might be on the way.
Now RAWMAN is doing something he
can't clearly ever remember doing

RAWMAN is praying.

12/95

OVERHEARD SONG

Chock full o' clock choked
understood at last;
merely half a pound of chopped chuck
handed over Bruno Kiskei style
wrapped in stiff white paper with the price
penciled in on the top.

All I had to do back then was pocket the change
and deliver it back around the corner.
Once it ticked upon your face
and the sound escaped upon your ears.

Now you try to force the black hands back.
And sing the song of the overheard in a red line
than sweeps so sure and smooth waves passing
in an inkling of the missed infinity.

The movement imperceptible impression
toward enviable destination.
Maybe some Novocain in November
Maybe not.

This would, however, move your ears, to sigh.
To believe this;
the texture in request
to abandon the selfish din
and when put to the question,
"Where is it have I been?"

Smile and nod and start with, "Listen...."

I would pull the fingers from deep in your ears
and lick the wax
Next whisper, "watch"
Then tune the tongue
in time to match.

6/92

OF CHANCES & POISON

After Four a.m. the streets went tracked over glass.
Pellets of ice lighted the icy sidewalks
like spent cartridges.

It was wind up time.
Across the recall ran silent pictures, more shadow, than story
shapes were there to interpret, but one did so at their own
risk. At last, there was the sound of the clicking of
spindles from the print leaving the housing, it was a relief.
Until the take up reel picked up speed and started to whip
and slap the black film in a hard fast circle.
Then you wanted at the plug.
In the silence, that eventually ensued, a dozen minor intents
conspired to murder each other in kind or without malice,
likewise no forethought or premeditation.
Judgement would pass like rented U-Haul trucks with
Vermont tags, bound for a cellar storage in Oswego.

The worst part of the feature to deal with, was the memory
and knowledge, that any and all of your exposure was just
undeveloped film. Once you shot it, everyone called it a wrap
and went home, to their own gibbets.
The conjecture and career talk back in the can.
Until the next time after four a.m. the streets were tracked
over glass and ice pellets littered the sidewalks
like spent cartridges.

Winter 85

HELLO BLUE MONDAY

The bartender was
like a thimble of wet light
in a long, dry, dark afternoon
in Maytag desert.
He offered yellow lined paper
in grey laundered matted Sunday streets.

Spring 85

AFTER THE NAP

There were juice stains on her lips. There were always juice
stains on her lips, it was a matter of just how purple
today, really, I thought. It was soon after the nap and she was
warm and puffy eyed. She padded into the room barefoot
on the coffee colored rug. Her brown hair yellow in the late
afternoon sunlight on loan form the first National Bank of
Bay Windows. It all hung in thick strands and mats like a
nest of stolen straw. She was freshly slept in. She had on
her Cabbage Patch Underwear and a torn striped shirt. She
came over to the chair holding a small white container of
Chicken McNuggets. I asked, "How's the corporate poison?"
She said, "Is not." I said, "Is too."
Is not. Is too. Is not. Is too. Is not. Is too.
This went on for awhile. "Look," I said, "it's corporate
poison, nothing against you, it just is, that's all."
I thought this would settle the issue. Wrong. "No, it's not,"
she said slightly annoyed, "It's Bicken McMuggets."
"Sure," I said, "THAT'S what they want you to THINK."
Then she sneezed violently. A thick green stream of mucus
shot out of her nose and hung down to her lips. It was very
nice. "Listen honey, " I said, "better pull yourself together."
She left the room quickly in tears, looking for someone to
wipe her nose.
And I thought "Damn, someday I'm going to learn how to
talk to women."

Spring 84

TAKE OLD 5

Only gets one channel: WSEE
Frito neon pigment pours hot lean cream
purples and oranges on white chilly sheets
great light to screw in,
turn the sound down. Ear to the carpet crackle
with a bushel full of static.
Just gone to sleep by the Lake.
No butter rolls No Drakes's Cakes
count my inventory in out of state plates.

Take old 5. West
Go drive into some nice little town.
Where they still say "hi ya" to you on the street.
After you cross the state line,
they call it the purple heart highway.
Next morning traditional blinding white blacktop is served.
Here is the wheel. Here are your hands.
I think you know where they both go.

So you're at work on time and freshly showered and
camouflaged.
Your file is on hand and I'm pouring gasoline on my
best gifts and in my mouth is this Ohio Blue Tip
as toothpick.
I'm grinning at you.
It's not a good grin.
You know, they say you can strike them anywhere.

City Motel Erie PA 90

WHERE IS LUCKY WARD?

Where is lucky ward tonight...is he out of cigarettes
or don't he need them anymore?

Is Hot Horse calling him up and in his best three
day drunk voice asking,
"Well, Hiya you old bastard, Why aren't you dead yet?
And if you were... how would you ever tell?"

"Dammit," he goes "...my phone don't ring for a week,
then I get three phone calls in an hour...two
wrong numbers and this.... I just don't see the difference.

All the rest of you smart ass bastards have got
machines to screen things out...Now I'll ask you what
have I got?"

The line went silent.
"S'matter, out of questions?"
Hot Horse could feel Lucky's grin in the receiver.
"Want news don't you...the details....divorce...infidelity
Drunken confessions..alibis ....bragging either how much
money I make or how much I owe...Well you can forget it."

The silence went on longer this time.
"Yikes," thought Hot Horse, "I only wanted to ask
how his kids were."

Then Lucky Ward said, "Keep away from me, there pal;
Don't know you anymore. Just too long ago to be bothered
digging up a bunch of old bones for a little leftover meat."
"Yeah, I remember you. So what. How'd you get this number
anyway, it's unlisted."

"Oh," said Hot Horse, "ran into an old friend of yours."
"Yeah, like who?" Lucky Ward is interested.

The silence went on and on and then clicked,
like the sound of old plastic faceplate's switch,
or gravel and dirt falling off a shovel followed by the dial
tone.

Now in the bar, it's Hot Horse who has the grin.

He's whispering, "Love that man."

2/91

MEMORY BOAT MORN

(For J.S.)

We are back here in the rear end
of an old morning
when the early summer morning sun
warmed the bricks in big wide
yellow sheets
My son lies on the red tile floor
amusing himself with twenty-five
bucks of plastic and decals.
His remark is, it's a cheap little truck
The ladders come off again, better drive
it to a gas station.

All this and more plays at my feet
this memory boat morning
soft, precious, fleeting totally
dependent upon my every thought and action;
recall has the ball at the moment
and the memory comes in between the
chin and the heart.
The heat is high and inside.
So I'll step out of the box and ask for time.

The bay's basin grows in
soft dawn color as the
tide laps the current
while two flat bottom ferries
criss-cross in ripples.

I'm at the shore line down
at the end of fourth street
with the windshield on my easel
packed with coffee and butts
a soft Parker on the tape
and a close friend at the elbow.

We watch the sun come up
and take a long whizz
on the beach and talk with
grey smokes in the corner of
our lips.
It's warm back in the car
alive with bright morning light
a shimmer and a shiver and a shudder
in a weary dizzy delight.

The streets show a stain of night water
like a shawl across the shoulders
a shadow up in the red fire escape over the alleyway. And we
know we spent the night like cheap wolf tickets in Jericho.

A tangle of black snakes over front street.
Concrete eels over first coffee ghosts
alive in the wild spirit of Paumanok
Wolfe's words raise incarnate wish
Don't we want to go home
back to the sound bluffs
sound salt adhered to the self
as a second skin.
Then we would roam the shoreline and
banks above the beach
where the condos haven't
mushroomed yet.

It would have to be in the park
up by the 67 steps
to a wishing well, sealed over with a
rough cement.
Down inside a small voice trapped still
with a father's face, framed with jet
black curly hair and a slim kind hand
slipped into his young son's grasp.
Here to this remembered patch of turf
where we dreamed and wished and looked
out over the Sound in every season.
Here we loved and fought and I humped
you in the soft warm dirt of an August midnight;
I saw your face swept clean at noon brilliant
sunshine and fresh off shore breeze. Your eyes
as big as saucers filled deep with nectar. Our
hands together on the soft long necked chalice,
alive with the sound of sighs at dawn.
We'll just lie down right here
near the edge of the cliffs
in the shade of pines.
Go get that blue blanket
out of the trunk.

January 90

THINGS THAT ARE.....

Smart toilet ducks
Hover Decade 90
Hot fruit and fiber cheese logs
Preventative reaction, Lucky strikes
Mint flavored spermicide
All of the turkey, none of the guilt beef jerky
Brent Mussburger
Camouflaged Condoms
Ferri Barbi
Coke spoon Ken
Sgt. Shock camp
Oat and raisin bran flavored bikini briefs
Pianosaurus
Nerf Ball Home pregnancy test
Durkee Dress all
Yacky Doodle
Microwaveable
Wink Martindude
Smurf's Aerobic Hour
Pollenex Ion Machine
Personal Iron Lung
She-Ra the Princess of Power
Your Daily accident forecast
The points of a thousand of Knuckleheads.

Summer 90

JEANIE

In a wide white lip grin she shook
her shoulder length brown blunt cut
in a slow, sure twirl that took forever
like a cat circling the house chasing her tail
around the foundation to the basement.

Her eyes like puzzles put to you before you were ready.
Now on this night a face and a memory that is like
a round tooth pick in a flat tooth jaw.
In this space between
time and flesh. The place of the smiles before
any knowledge the delayed fuse
and all these Barley grenades,
that go off in ticks and recurring
dreams and lips barely brushed.
This lush night with running hot and cold whispers
the shy side glance of eternity softsliding things
that keep the back lit.

Jeanie plays on the floor at Nannie's house
with me as Ben walks over us to look down,
careful not to step on us.

I can still see your legs swinging under the trays
foil peeled off halfway with fresh steam
over TV dinners in silver aluminum autumn
at five with the Rangers in the first period
at the old garden.

I heard once she became a Nurse.
Hey, Jeannie, remember the time you and Mary Ann
rubbed the poison oak all over yourselves to get
out of school?
It worked, didn't it?

I still itch.

                                        July 90

LIST ODD POEMS

1.
2. Thunderstorm in April saying yes and no at the same time.
3. Indian spinning in a drying machine pretending it's a
   spaceship.
4. Television eating smaller televisions.
5. Film clips of war in which the aircraft all have wooden
   propellers.
6. Man furiously banging the steering wheel of a car the
   instant before impact.
7. General population of small mid-western city glad because
   they can walk.
8. Woman being forced to sing in the shower with strange man.
9. Grenadier rowing on the Thames with buckets on his hands.
10. Black and white B-52's opening bomb bay doors over
    Plattsburgh at Easter time.
11. Yellow back-hoe with a mouth full of dirt at dawn.
12. Three locals at corner tavern up at the front of the bar
    drinking beer and listening to the door.
13.

Winter 91

KNOCKING YOURSELF OUT

I go in this joint called
"The purple Porpoise.'
I'm gonna eat some oysters
and eat french fries and
drink a little beer.
I sit down at the bar. I order up. So I'm drinking a little beer.
I'm looking for something to do,
while I'm waiting for the food.
There's a couple across the room in a booth.
They're real cozy. Ain't love grand I think.
She's strikingly attractive.
He's a regular guy.
They have their heads together.
She's grinning at me.
I grin back.
The regular guy makes a face.
She thinks I don't know she's jerking him off under the table.
Just then the food is set in front of me.
I ask for some salt and pepper to go with the FF's and oysters.
The bartender comes back with
three pepper and two salt shakers.
"Knock yourself out," he says.

84

UNTITLED

You said the color combination affixed the white washed
    moved.
    If that was indeed the case

I should have kept pliers handy
    To squeeze the seconds longer
                    And hold the corduroy stationary.

Twenty times a solitary shrill wail
reverberated shattering the dream of sleep

            I resisted, then insisted...upon fantasy.

Box cars lurch in my dreams where in
once we held each other to muffle
and soothe that cry of objects and products
shuttling from the windowless warehouse to warehouse.

The more laden with freight
    the more intense the weight
            Tremble the very heart's foundation
                    Shake a precarious emotional state.

You said the crystal irises of the eyes
    were So Reflective
            By the dark rings rim
                    Are measured the process
                            Of elimination.

Bellingham WA 78

SCREWING ME THROUGH SCHENECTADY

December was as sad as what was left of Utica
around the train station platforms.
All the ghosts that never got the good jobs at G.E.
Now porter in limbo vapor luggage about shattered pillars.

So when he showed up and identified himself as
a recorder third class, representing the Bureau of
Alcohol, Tobacco and Red Meat all the apparitions
scrambled for his luggage and called him sir.

The fullness and bounty in the quality of life he was
leading was so apparent.
What a knee slapper.

He dreamed of calibrating all the volume control presets
of the Amtrak couch intercoms.
So he could purr out the stops along the Hudson from the
speakers suggesting each station was where each passenger
had always dreamed of getting off at one day.

It would be like screwing you through Schenectady.
Or maybe just saying it a lot.
Slowly as the ruins slide by.
You'd be just mounting the thigh.

Sliding the ruins slowly by.
The least you could have
admitted to me once
it might had been worth
giving it a try.
So slide the ruins slowly by
screwing me through Schenectady.

12/92

SMALL TIME CHEAP GREEK TRAGEDY

Contemporary Directory and Writer's Program

Now you too can compose plays for the stage for the ages. Easy to follow topical suggestions makes the creative process a snap.

Select from Menu below:

A. Tormented lover dismembers her lover's genitals.

B. Sons murder parents for inheritance.

C. Mother drowns infant sons.

D. Prominent Gladiator slits the throats of estranged lover and rival.

(These programs come complete with eager ready-made immense audiences of vacant garbage addicted celebrity obsessed citizenoids that will greet your genius with showers of money and devotion.)

And if you act immediately we will include with

your order for the Small Time cheap Greek Tragedy
Contemporary Directory and Writer's Program
these plausible and useful possible future plot
outlines and scenarios for the Year 2000.

1. As Millennium period draws to a close,
paranoid culture slips into collective psychosis
and apocalyptic religious and race war ensues.

2. Popular game show hosted by powerful politician
popularizes social security number lottery through
patriotic demagogy to incite global inquisition.
Lucky winners are skinned and tanned and put on
public display. Surviving family members get weekend
vacation in Las Vegas.

3.Aliens return during half-time at the Super Bowl.
They announce that after much discussion the high
Inter-Galactic council has decided that effective
immediately all money, clothes, and electricity
will vanish from earth indefinitely.
Crowd thinks it's part of the entertainment.

Stadium goes black. Buffalo still loses to Tampa Bay.

11/94

RAIN DATE

(For R.B.)

Sheldon had rainout in his eyes
as he told me, " I met Mantle once, he was a monster, I asked
for his autograph in Times Square and he knocked me down."

It continued to rain steadily.
Then an usher appeared, newspaper under his arm heading
for the subway platform. This was not good.
Sheldon and I exchanged worried glances.
I could still see Mantle knocking him down in Times Square.

Just before noon, the beat-up
blue P.A. system, mounted near the
entrance gates barked some barely
intelligible garble about calling
everything off, rain checks, regrets, etc.
the message was repeated over
and over. Sheldon got the message. I turned to watch his
back grow smaller in the grey parking lot.

I felt as if something had physically been taken from me.
Everything started to deflate. There was the sound of air
     hissing from
the P.A. speakers. I walked by a Sheik selling the post. From
his white robes, he gave me the evil eye. Then he hissed,
     "Shibboleth."

This was another bad sign. I thought either all this was my
    fault or
I had disemboweled his children. Maybe he thought I was
the one who knocked Sheldon down in Times Square.

The speakers had stopped hissing.
They said it had been merely a
corporate decision, loss leaders,
advance sale, early in the year, why
risk million dollar tax structures on soggy April sod?
Sure the skies were only Queen's mist now, but it had rained
hard the night before, a lot of the players had hangovers
So I just walked in circles around the stadium,
trying not to look at all the disappointed children,
wishing that something would change,
that someone would realize a terrible mistake had been made.

It was like having the concrete of the platform of the Number 7
evaporate under your feet.

It shouldn't have ended this way.
All that life and excitement, just called off.

Later on the bus, I thought about how many years already it
had been since Richard had been dead.
And I wondered, if where he is now, does he sleep in a room
that smells like cigarettes all night?

92

L.I. SOUND

Now in this past of a punched ticket
at low tide I drink down this July sun.
Cathedral afternoon of canopy blue
in an endless awning sky;

Myself looking at the sealed plastic bag
of fiddler crabs as bait
thinking how hot and doomed it was inside
there.

Now after the rituals were observed
and completed nude solitary on the beach
Walking as elderly on the thousand stones
toward the water
wanting into the cold salty stinging sound
Your balls drawn up into a hard sphere
The waves at your ass the erect nipples
the water licking everything in degrees at once.

The excitement from the prospect
of entering her as she enters you.
These ten years past her flesh now sea better yet sound
Under this sky, bright bare to the shoreline shoulder

I'm dunking. Going under. Full immersion. Opening my
eyes underneath. The pressure of the silence has its
tongue in my ear. I'm coming up for air. I push off
and explode in high white foam.

I look back on the beach
to see who is lying under the makeshift driftwood
lean-to as the Sound breeze chops the darker blue
waters white while fluttering the contour sheet
in animated penciled in ripples.

And I recall falling into your eyes that moment
and never looking down
still finding I never, ever hit the bottom.
Even now.

7/91-2/93

CHINESE NEW YEAR

Missing you from the marketplace I grow lonely.
This Winter sings crystals heaped upon the handrail
that is soaked with urine.
It evaporates the snow in a steamy hiss of your exile.
In the vapor is the knowledge I should not see soon
your face at my door.

While my chest is tight
I dwell on a smile in the bright moon of July.
We speak in the shadows
sentimental affairs of a private ear.

Each day I recall this.
The season sings a different name.
At night a dream washes its face
to reveal the promise beneath
that goes from day to day disguised.

In the bleakness that greys.
The blind eye that excludes.
For your ear the ordinary cork.

But the light in the eyes that was extinguished
could hope to be flame recalled.
Without accident.
Our time awake more punctuated with humiliation than
periods of hours given to simple sleep.

If you could find that bliss in slumber.
In that your face could provide
those gentle illusive arms that did embrace
to melt the touch that day to day did efface.

So it's time to take off your clothes
in this chilly uncertain prose
and lie with me
as the wind neglects
to kiss your neck
and put you to bed.
Without the word
better left sadly unsaid.

2/94

BARS ON THE CAGE

Nailed in Perkins
to a hangover full blast
to the booth next to an
impossible Wednesday morn;
A bully of blue sky bright
shaking fist in your face;
going, "Good Morning You Asshole."
All you can do is sit there.
Wary on an angle cross legged
hiding behind dark glasses
and saying, "So far, so good."
Rather than all this being odd or scary
you find it a relief and refreshing.

Here in the shrouded Sunrise from Ames.
So light a little poison..
The spark looks like some bastard dwarf
being forced to copulate with Snow White
merely because they had a go at her.

My team of waitresses are
maternal and attentively gentle
Such consideration. Why not?
I look like I just rolled
A Serento Cheese tractor trailer.

In the big Plate glass
is framed your vision for the day.
This big sign poised on the business end
of Seventy five feet of slim tapered
brown six inch thick steel; with a
footing that goes down nine feet.

On the zenith
it reads "GET N' GO"
O.K. by me I think,
but I thought this was a SPECIAL OCCASION
as a beaten looking teenager
rubs the carpet sweeper's
nose into it.

3/90

LIFESTYLES

Lifestyles of the poor and unknown
Victor gets up about 5:30 every morning.
He usually feels like shit.
The only thing he can think about is coffee.
Depending on where it is
that he wakes up, it could take him as long as an hour and a half to
get enough change for coffee. Victor fits in rather well with the
morning rush of yuppies at the coffee shop.
If Micky's in a good mood
the coffee cup will be bottomless for a couple of hours. Last week a
system analyst from Larchmount, who used to listen to Emerson,
Lake and Palmer bought him a Stella D'oro Breakfast treat.

Lifestyles of the young and trendy.
Marie say's she's "tired of cocaine." She has been losing a lot of
weight.. Just the other day she microwaved
some Banquet Weight Watcher
Gourmet pizza toast and then didn't want any. She put it in the
refrigerator and heated it up in the toaster oven for breakfast the
next day. It gave her the runs.
She has been late for work three times this week.
The other girls in the office are starting to talk.

Lifestyles of the common and tragic
Doug had sat in the same bar, in the same seat,
for about five years.

He said the same sort of things most of the time. He talked about
his job. He didn't like his boss. Sometimes he shaved. Other times
he didn't. As a rule he drank up most of his money.
His big joke is to tell others at the bar that his life is "a living hell."
He doesn't know it yet, but he has cancer of the colon.

Lifestyles of the beat and ridiculous
Ocean (not his real name) has just finished his 15th chapbook of
unpublished poetry. He keeps writing about this great artist he'll
just never be. He doesn't have the guts
or the smarts or talent to get
his work published and feels that this counts for some sort of artistic
integrity. The gleam that was once in his eyes has seen better days.
He has drifted, drunk and sulked over the same endemic turf
up and down the coast for any
number of years now, not in the least bit
closer to where he once thought he was going.
Last time anyone heard he was studying to be
a fireman in San Francisco.

Lifestyles of the drunk and dangerous.
Jack perched his elbows at the bar. It was happy hour target time.
Jack caught some guys eye and shot him his best menacing
demonstrative grin, "SO ASSHOLE ARE YOU PART OF A CLUB
OR SOMETHING OR DID YOU THINK
IT UP ALL BY YOURSELF TO DRESS UP LIKE THAT?"
Then Jack farted loudly and slammed
his beer glass shattering it on the bar.
While the glass and foam were still very much in the air,
Jack bolted forward and in mid air grabbed hold of the guy's tie,
knocking him to the floor. Jack was now straddling him.
(In a technique hulk Hogan might have admired)
 While sitting on his victim's chest, tie in one fist,
the jagged bottom of the glass

in the other, Jack's tone turned conversational, "So...wanna lock horns or tangle assholes?"

88

NOTHING CONSTRUCTIVE

There was nothing constructive again.
I just looked out in the garage
and the leftover rage looked back
and said nothing constructive

You had the late October
flipped open to the Autumn
with the yellow light
late afternoon
the piano soft touch
keys to another volume

Next store around noon
your neighbor took
one swing by the house
riding red tractor drunk

You hoped he wouldn't jackknife
instead
He disappeared
into the nothing constructive
from last summer
he just never took in.

The sound of a man
speaking out of turn.

Or was that place.
Somewhere between
having to eat shit
with a smile
and
about ready to invite
you over for a bite.
Of course we are talking dinner here,
my dear.

I've got nothing constructive for you.
Somewhere beyond the hissing fits
the smug bravado
the bile bright name calling
the dirty looks that lasted two years.

To quote Ron Swoboda; "Why am I putting so much
effort into such a mediocre career?"

So now shriveled ferns dance blind in that gold light
bent into musical notes that sway in the wind singing
nothing constructive.

                                        10/93

COUNTY FAIR

In the hot dust and early evening light
there was this grim face of the man
who ran the merry go round.

Stuck in the running middle of the apparatus
Stooped, round shouldered,
he kept his eyes averted toward the ground.

As the whole damn thing spun around him.

Periodically, between rides, he looked slant eyed
side to side for the only two sounds he understands.

One's the all clear
and time to set the gate back into place.

So he climbed past the mothers and children
perched some askew sidesaddle wooden horses
with frozen grimaces in the heat.

Then the circles slowly started to a crawling that
twisted tighter and he gradually released the
lever the whole greased grotesque
monstrosity moved with a life
of its own.

I stood there and watched it go past me.
Every so often I caught the face of my lover and
my child as they went round and round.

At the hand of a tired man
with a beaten face.
His hand releasing a lever.
And he catches your eye
and mouths out the words
while slowly shaking his head from side to side.
"Don't lose your grip."

6/91

ICY BLUE DRIVE

On that which was smothered in grey and white,
our path worn in an icy blue, as we drove away.
The slightest heel applied
a little too soon
touch too hard
or too fast
and you would be spinning out of control.
No brakes on this one;
you're going to have to steer out of this.

You in the black dress
the high heels and your hair still wet
from the shower.

All I could think of was
what would it all do first.
Steam or freeze?

Certainly the ice everywhere.
Every curb coated in a straight jacket of mirrors.

You had translated my words into another language
I clearly didn't understand;
but liked the way you spoke
the tongue in that husky whisper.

Sitting next to me in the car that afternoon
on your way to dinner at the teacher's table
I was left in charge of the brakes
and the wheel and the defroster.

We started out somewhere between thin ice and glare ice.
Every movement since has been intersection after
intersection ablaze in green and yellow lights.

Little has changed since
till that one
night I bolted awake out of that same dream
all covered in red.

Winters 91/93

MY MIRAGE MISTRESS

(For J.W.)

In the door she comes
all dolled up in red and black.
Two parts Diana Riggs to one part able yeoman.
My ears and eyes fight over the sirens
as feet shuffle for foothold.

Her laughter in the next generation of another Star Trek
or was that Star Search?
And popping a little speed she says catching your breath
"good to see you."

I say, "You are wearing the colors that cover my windows."
Her smile collapses under your feet and don't that spin
beneath any entrance befitting a dream give ground.

Where in last night
on the pillow asleep in this chimera
next to me fast asleep
in this gush of black hair and thick wide wish
lips to full cheeks.
I could only watch.
Knowing this dream; as in, if you reach for,
all will vanish, either way.

And we might have spoken of maps at midnight
but the hour, seldom right as may have been once,

Has evaporated to become vapor.

"It's devil water," the boys shout.
While the smell of hamburgers fills the bar real familiar.
Over green little bottles of drained rolling rocks
And what they can't say is,
"Never let it be said I was not fully aware
of the slippage and the damage as it went down,
and it was drinking with purpose as opposed to,
drinking with no purpose.
And when the morning after forced a common distinction
there was little comfort in waking alone.

And she is back upon the black road with her fingers
guiding the wheel between dream lines of yellow and white.
Thinking, "That went fast."
"He tried to dance with me and then he just disappeared."

I remember hugging you in October at the door
and your dress and underwear got cinched up

                                        October 91

UNTITLED

Fast eyes fish for hook wives
across a nearby parking lot.
Dusk arrives giving only
a look at the undersides.
And you found yourself agreeing
even though you don't think so.

Then you're left with your ass in the air banking on
milking the horizon for all that it's worth.
All the news in scraps roll reflected templates
dejected the Harbor Master started concern for the
like's of port and starboard..
And everybody else's bad habits;
hunger and thirst; fornication and defecation
On the corner the word from the bullhorns
is EVACUATE...EVACUATE...

It's more than the manner of your annunciation
this time. Forget your ethics. Save the ethic playing acting.
Fuck you and your etymology.

Such nice language.
In what tongue are they tied up now.
Reclined on big pillows of past
no words here just a slow sure flip over pages
gone fan by now another fading map.
Middle age nap time beckoning at noon
from the dull light hung about the

walls as naked frames full of promises
so a silent film projected..
What was going on in the mind's eye?
Can we remember our favorite lines when it's time?

Then this scene when the word was clear and long
and not the center for focus.
Just pictures.
The walls were white tail seats hard molded butt bucket
hard marble green.
The coffee in her hands was in a white plastic cup.
I showed how to nip out the corner of the lid like
contractors do.
The train was on time.
Whose eyes did the longing?

Whose boots did the heel toe?
Considering how time has moved in the fabric
of recall.

Not like here in the present
the one you fear the best
like it was never an issue
just another disposable guest.

6/92

SO, WHERE WERE YOU?

Watching the clock
thinking, "she'll be coming round the mountain,
when she comes."
And it is "The thrill is gone" as done by Stan Kenton.
It just crushes them out
one by one
and you're hunting toothpicks in the woods.

So go ahead   such a big sport.
Put your ass   in a sling
and when the boot comes
hope to god   it still swings

So where will the wild roads row?
Inasmuch as:
one in the can
one with his truck his dog
on an interstate dropping South.
One in rehab on the mend.
One sits at home under house arrest
with the studio audience.
One is banished thoroughly. (To everyone's satisfaction)
One fresh in the ground.

Off night clock watch
makes me wish I was born a lefty;
might have made a difference
at least...in shadow control.

This is just what comes to mind
at a glance: your best blank stare
on the tip of your tongue
you used to be able to taste it on your lips.

This one, he empties his pockets
night after night
like a box of Cracker Jacks
hoping for a prize.
(He hasn't gotten yet or he could still recognize)

So how many faces will it take you tonight?
And you wanted them clockwise; right or was
that counter then to...just what version was this?

Common variations in search of theme
and there's the clock on the wall
all hands always tall pointing towards something
far away or simply not yet.

The white face in the boneyard
where the well is ordinarily pretty dry.

Fall 94

ONE SHOT

Yeah, you get one shot to stop the room.
There will be no competition, while the in-house
comedians and secretaries gossip at the bar whos
got the latest case of AID's or the old stand-by
cancer. You of course had the attention span of
lint. Nobody's blaming you, after all the operant
conditioning to Huckleberry Hound and Fruity Pebbles
wishing still that just once the rabbit would get those KIXX.
This is truth. As regrettable as that sounds. Here's
shrugging at you kid. Too bad about those dreams being
blanderized right down to size. Do you remember the day
you just didn't wake up and all your expectations had been
mutilated and miniaturized. Another creamed dream.
Where the radio goes off the air, for the last time and the
noise in the air goes white and the static stayed hot
for a half life of seventy years. Not a test pattern to spare.
Maybe you can live under that satellite dish..dig a tunnel
out. And it's why listen to this..the newest reason in the
book; because it too is in your face, without the benefit
of a publicity campaign, corporate incentives, cash rebates
this will not soft soap your ass, lube your G-spot, coddle
your fears, cup your breast, hold your head up, retrace
your footsteps. This is just what it sounds like. I'm pissed
off, scared to death, malformed and between four day drunks
and the same old tired routine. The angry man at the micro-
phone stand. The voice in the shopping center wilderness
marked down, reduced, half off, slightly damaged in shipping
warning tags removed, attitude like industrial strength

dragon pus, come on waltz around the room with me, I'm
your worst fuckin' nightmare and favorite B-movie script
and I'm here with the consequences; the test results;
the air tight alibis, the crying towels, the wailing walls
Microsoft meatball hero recipes, here with the S&L hearings
of T-Bills wolf tickets. White collar crime
in concentration camp pajamas .Thirty something Newspeak
for Dow Industrials, can you smell those bearings heating
up of the conglomerate corporate combined with big black
sharp blades just humming your way.
Not with products, but ideas, stageflats, grease paint,
30 second fixed rate visions
the dancing lessons, a new diet plan just back from space
with John Hinckley select a target color coded meal planning
cards, complete with the disenfranchised obsession of choice.
The voice of the second. I'm doing it all with mirrors and
smoke. If you should hear anything familiar; see anyone you
might know. Remember I'm doing it
with mirrors and microphones.
And guess in what direction it points tonight. And that voice
you hear runs like clockwork in everyone's head.
Just the voice of a second. Over and out.

                                        Summer 90

TWO TERSE PIECES OF CORRESPONDENCE FROM CALIFORNIA

(For K and S)

Wednesday afternoon when I got home from the
Lake Side Warehouse I received two terse pieces
of correspondence from California.

One was from a girl I used to know.
We once had a short forgotten minor league affair
twenty years ago in our home town.
We were both quite young and didn't know love from a
bag of Fritos.
We are both married now,
and live on opposite ends of the country.
We had been writing to each other again.
Her letter was written on
Northern California Mortgage & Loan stationery,
that's heading stated in blue bold print:

Things to do.....TODAY

1. Is that what you wanted to hear?
2. Are we all square now?
3. Did you want anything else?

4. Whose grave is that?
5. You already knew how I felt about you.
6. Tell me a good story.

The second letter was from the editor of a
defunct literary magazine who was once good enough
to print one of my poems.

He thanked me for the tape I had sent him and the
bulk of the half page letter went:

"It's been a while since I wrote or heard from you.
Lots has happened here. Moved form Santa Maria to the
foothills of the Sierra in Northern CA. Then in a huge
December storm a 100ft. Cedar crashed though the roof of
our house and landed in bed next to me.
Fortunately my wife was out of town and
I was sleeping on her side of the bed
and thus walked away without a scratch. So I get a second
chance. But my car (parked just outside) was totaled
(and uninsured) and the house is still unliveable.
And so it goes...."
Then one day
the letters from California
just stopped.

3/96-5/96

UNTITLED

Her face at the train station in Glen Cove.
Afternoon grey, muggy lush.
You between the coaches
poised for the cinematic farewell
as the train pulled out of the station
She in tears running after you
her features collapsing
from the pull of the diesel.

Over and over
that scene runs
these rails endlessly.

Her tough little profile
the fine fragile features
the heave of those minuscule breasts
under your V neck tee shirt
that she refused to take off after you and she
had made love back at the house just before leaving.

Now it's across a hard dirty track bed
where she lays her form down next to the
steel rails that disappeared
into the nowhere that became you.

Summer 80

SKIP THE GUTTER

And then one day
winter starts coughing up
bits of spring.
In the beaten curbs
garnished in a smear of fetid mud clots
and it all looks so very freshly hacked up.

At the wheel just before noon
your eye catches her form shrouded in dust
strolling along the edge of the road
just insolently enough off the curb.
To pull your glance into the slit
of the rear view mirror.

Yes, there she is all dolled up
in black from head to toe
from the cape to the heeled boot
being propelled along like a
fragment of torn paper ripped out from
a fashion supplement,
just blowing down the gutter.

And you wonder
will spring come this year
to all those sullen faces
at the wheel
trying to skip the pot holes
that the snowplows dug

looking out from the ruts
that they all insist upon
living in.

Spring 96

MY KIND OF MORNING AFTER

I've skinned my knuckles
out on the driveway
late last night.
Now my socks are halfway
down in my boots.
Fly the flag at half mast.
I'm thinking of you.

Fall 96

ORDINARY ROAR

July will linger just near the door
as it is time now to go
and in a sigh or perhaps that ordinary roar
inform the waning afternoon in the calendar's
numerical voice that your number is up.
What startles you with all its whispering are
concussions that wake the waves to break
and break over the short eroded rocky bug infested
disappearing shoreline.

I hear strange voices in this ardent insistent wind.
I feel a tongue just inches from my ear that speaks
'in that sigh or ordinary roar that after all these years I
was assured I wouldn't be able to hear anymore.
All about this hazy animation of dirty white foam
driven madly on and upon.
So parade a succession of walkers across the face in
the beach. They nod or speak appearing as apparitions
that drift windblown on the most silent of feet.
Only some will find the courage to speak.

Scraps of paper and fragments of prose difficult to define
whip by in a helpless driven fury.
Now expression has little opportunity for introspection
or reflection. The art of language has been lost in
the stiff insistence of a brisk lake gust of wind.
And the sky above is so blue and blank
and it's almost like time herself has slipped out

of her harness and has run on the shoreline
riding on the wind, being blown all over the beach
naked, wild and free of the sigh or that ordinary roar
of us as July lingers near the calendar's door.

7/95

APPLIANCE MODE

(For F.F.)

No, I won't rant or rave tonight or offend or threaten like
a big bad energizer psycho-scare bunny, still going and
going after all these years still refusing to disappear,
vanish into detox, rehab, remanded into the custody of the
proper authorities, muzzled, silenced by encroaching middle
age, vague cow eyed indifference or small time community
college academic snobbery.
Around still.....dripping with deadly cholesterol
habits and cheap greasepaint offering to share a spot of
soft flesh verbal carpet bombing trauma while my puss
spits tobacco and cheap watery beer expecting you to
regard all this with the same reverence reserved for
the sacraments of forgotten decorum, and protocol.

Yes, for tonight only I will repent. Offer real serious
important poetry. I'll take a crack at rewriting T.S.
Eliot like, "In the mall, the bitches come and go
drooling over Leonardo Dicaprio." Or I suppose that
The Waste Land could use a contemporary make-over,
"Fox is the cruelest network mingling derivative
mediocrity with a calculated cynicism to elevate the
common denominator to new levels of debasing crude desire."

Or better yet tonight I will adjust my attitude to ooze
a low fat, high fiber pus that when it anoints the forehead
of consumers of all types and ages; the normal and demented;

the preferred customer co-star or walk on extras with
rejected social political affiliation....All will be
brought to salvation at last. To the place where the
living waters of sound financial investments and positive
cash flow will be a baptism at the hands of young maidens
shining the brilliant laser red razors of electronic
cash registers ringing up explosions of unit priced coded
epiphanies....All will be delivered, transformed into
model citizen-zoids; politically correct citizenzoids
bland emotion-less indifferent passion-less greedy
beyond the power of thought or speech or self-expression
other than to convey desire and lust for name brands.

Yes, that's what I will do tonight; forget the poetry;
pathos; prose and roses, I will reflect what everyone
really seems to want... I'll just stand up here and
describe useless indulgent consumer products. I will
transform myself into the home-shopping network of
creative prose/poetry expression commodity:

Tonight only!!! European style driving gloves lined
with imported gray ranch rabbit. DE-lux T.V. feature den
pole mounted gyro-balanced with built in center of
gravity lava-lamp; comes in puce, milk or mauve;
yes hurry; supplies are...of course...limited.

Next comes the enchanting neo-jet trash polyester
starlight crepe exercise jump-suit. You'll be the envy
of your fringe hate group with the marvelous mohair
poncho heart shaped accident rug. Proudly display your
solid brass cricket, symbol of good luck and hospitality,
Centipede shoe rack, and teeny tiny all-electric fry boy.
You need those scented boot stuffers, all weather dog, cat
pet taxi. Why this golf bag converts into luggage with
a flick of the wrist. Silk Chrysanthemums circuit breakers

choke hold chukka boots. Did I hear you say we need more
"brass"? Well...take a gander...at those solid brass
mallard hooks. They're darling. As are the solid brass
door knockers, solid brass adult diaper safety pins.
Do you realize you could have your family name spelled
out proudly on your front lawn in series of sunny little
foot and a half porcelain duckies captured in mid-goose
step. Turn chaos into charm with your very own
computerized Swedish stainless steel corn on the cob
holders which double as satin eraser clothespin
disinfectants.

So you see no more ranting. Tonight is the last time.
From now on I'm not rantin...I'm rooting!
Come root with me. Root! Root tootin robots!
This is a wonderful world full of wonderful products
to shop for. Let's think 'good" thoughts. Remember the
special times. All through the little towns with everything
as holy and peaceful as on Superbowl Sunday morning.
It's like being invited to dinner on Gilligan's Island
with the howls. Sssshhhh! There up on the screen
corporate America's moving its bowels. At 1,000,000
dollars per thirty second commercial spot
is it not time to remember a simple, gentler time.
It's time that we all take a moment to remember the
true meaning of Superbowl Sunday Years ago dad used
to gather us kids around the small tiny black and white
TV with the bent twisted hanger antenna in the
tattered living room and repeat a simple prayer. We sat
in respectful silence with our heads bowed till the
stillness was broken by one of us kids who would ask,
"Dad....who ya rooting for?"

And in that quiet strong voice he would say, "Kids,
I'm rooting for the happy people, the gentle folk, those

peaceful sweet sentimental men who run our country with
such care, insight and wisdom. I'm rooting for all the
wise commentators and color men who with those generous
corporate sponsors enrich, define and regulate our
lives and aspirations in such a dignified, meaningful,
concerned, caring, rich and holy way.
Yea, verily they truly know what is best for us and we
should get down on our knees and humbly thank them for
the grace and beauty, the unbridled pagentry of living
this rewarding, sound modern fulfilling life.
And as for that little "game" down there on the field,
well let's just say, we need to see beyond that.
Yes kids I root for the good, those who are the strong
and who are the trusted."
And Mamma's tears would be streaming down her cheeks as
she softly sobbed, "Jim, that's beautiful, I love it when
you quote from Elvis."

This Appliance mode has been brought to you by....
YOU.......who bought it, who live it, who perpetuate it.

So for your penance: Go watch six major car commercials,
purchase three personal care products
and make a good corporate act of contradiction.

Go now...
And buy it no more.

Fall 88
Spring 92
Winter 98

THE YEAR THE EARTH SPOKE BACK

Your touch detonated her center
like a mushroom cloud
tucked between clean cold sheets
and when she came
there was this whistle in the wind
and her after-shocks shook the bedroom
like black and white declassified government
footage of a 1952 New Mexico test zone.

Winter 84

UP ON HOLLY AVENUE

She could heave under the cortisone
as if her thighs were driven by a metronome.
Well before the morning fog
fresh in from Bellingham Bay
consented to be burned off and give way
to a harbor montage set in wet varnish
as the dawn leaked out
from under the islands swollen to
black-eyed lumps
puffed upon the horizon.

Sullen over coffee at breakfast
she looked at him and asked,
"Just what do you look for in your women anyway?"
Without batting an eyelash he answered,
"defects."

Fall 78

THE SOUTH FORK OF SOMEWHERE

Do remember that summer afternoon
you picked me up on that beach
like a stray sea shell that amused you
and took me back to your attic apartment.

Your hair was red, mine yellow
we made a lot of orange that July.

79

NEW SUFFOLK

Just you and me in the back seat
of my 1963 Impala groping each other
while a grey bay light kept insisting,
"Don't worry...I'll just open windows a crack,
I won't start the car."
But very soon the rear windows are three-quarters
of the way down your legs and the power steering
wheel is itching and pulling for guiding hands.
We knew the best dead end road in the world.
And what it was for.
Never will shake your glistening grin
as I put the damn ignition key in.

78

UNTITLED

Voice is what is heard and recalled.
Chaos and noise those loveable predictable twins
serve as whores of the lazy spirit.
Then let me speak from the cusp of this night
less than ten above Zero on Herr Fahrenheit.
Moved by contemporary contrivances I stand naked ears
from the lands of sheriffs on patrol ever vigilant to
provide protection and shame in equal measure
as in just doing my job sir.

In this wonderful festoon you wish for yonder Fedayeen to
show and provide vision or at least a soundtrack with joke
that we can dance to.
But all the proper authorities ask is, "can you recite that
alphabet backward?
.....or maybe just walk that straight line."
Such damaged goods. Pray tell
was it shattered in shipping?
After all it is a simple request.
We don't ask much. However, when we do...well...you can
well understand our position as well as yours.
Prone and certainly dependent.
Your vulnerability is our meal ticket.

All I can come up with is
go and eat your vanilla in some other part of Valhalla

This night twists dawn's camisole askew
Exposing one hard brown nipple frozen brittle
Wanna see?
Or maybe just have a whiff.
Either way you take your pick while on the waltz
over towards the jeweled vowel cliff.

So it's Venus verbatim flytrap perched on the veranda.
Looking down
Later for you.

Feb 92

AIR SLANG

It happens every flag day.
It started with his foot.
It wanted to do the jazz nurse on the jaywalk to hell
There Jesse James gets to meet Aaron Burr.
(Or was that Raymond Burr?)
Narration by Vincent Price.

"Ah waits beep a light," he drawled
As the new Nazis from the same old Mars
ordered drinks and settled in for the millennium.

"Stinkers honkers sick spentz," one tells the other
in a stage side whisper.

All my knowledge knows but five shortcuts.
Don't worry.
You're not one of them.
Not in the middle of my worst day
could I abdicate from the vice squad
of stain patrol.

"Air snow full lie can knoll full," crackled out of
the scanner.

See here you crazy moron.
Saturdays are not for nothing

Satan gets off at ten.
And Sailor, where's your boat?

Or is this, "Return of the Magnificent Seven Little Dwarfs?"
And which one are you?

"But tune toot a gather," sang Richard the third on second.
Clint Walker squinted his eyes and
started to get a little pissed.
"Ah don need this shit," he snarled at the wardrobe
department's memo concerning future dry cleaning.

So in the Valley of Insolence,
the chant went up, "Burden hen swart tuna push."
Steak and legs, wild leeks
Zoo for rent, at last sea biscuit speaks,
"Butter laid den ever."

11/93

IN OCTOBER WHEN THE PRICE WAS RIGHT

Outside that night sounded like
they were moving the whole damn thing
by engaging deep gears to grind.
While gyrating iron teeth to filings
drained lubricants dry for thick couplings
deliberately pulling something apart in the darkness.

There is the smell of diesel fuel everywhere.
It almost works.
Now if there's no sparks... we're in business.

The faces watching, glow vacantly, flushed with excitement
of actually being in the studio audience.
The camera pans slowly the entire length of the raisers.
Squeals of gaiety as wireless microphone is passed
around and everyone got a chance to identify themselves,
where they were born and one special shallow wish.

When the red light clicked off.
The stage hands reappeared with the bull whips
and the host pulled back a lever and that sound
and that smell filled the room once more.

If it hadn't been for that short in the applause sign...
The price would still be right.

10/92

THE BOOK SCOUT

(For P.S.)

So where is the music in that old face?
The filthy red and grey
knitted wool beret that he wore when
he watched you run past the paper weight factory,
the tombstone show room.
First, as a child led by your father's hand
and then your son by your hand.
So when he offered his own,
a meat hook, leathered beet weathered brown
arthritic swollen rutabaga fingers,
you shook on the corner of the Cornet.

In his eyes he spoke,
"and what of all that easy conversation
......where did all that go?"
Here where the post modern meets local color
and forgets their lines and just repeats,
"nothing here, that's the shame,
you left the usual useless stain."

Don't sing about the past
with the scenery all
switched around off key;
to kiss the ass
of some "old time who used to be."

Whose only claim to fame
would appear to be that they are still alive
out on the great sad sidewalk earth.

And now for my part,
I get the chair
in the beat, cluttered little bookstore.
Forever in the cup of coffee
and still being allowed to smoke right inside.
To sit and read with the Ukrainian violins
mysteriously providing theme music.

So softly roll in and repeat the questions
and I on cue, will make the practiced replies
and we can drift to our somewhere else
by ourselves or in each others eye's.
What we know of our places will have to
be left on dusty shelves
and in forgotten volumes.
Right near that corner
where they don't look so much anymore.

I'll be waiting near the door.

9/93

WHAT PASSES BETWEEN

Look into my eyes
he said at quarter to three.
She saw a kind of brave shame
mixed in a bloodshot brown and green.
He looked back into her eyes
and saw a door open ajar.
From a crack under the jamb
a yellow cream
spilt onto the bed
and then something passed between.

Look into my ear
he whispered
see beyond bloodshot brown and green.
How could you know
where I have heard
and the things that I have seen.
Could you understand the time
I have passed between.
There was once another at the door
looking down the stairs
to the cellar where a furnace
heated the room.

Can feel the warmth which is now light
that slowly fills this room
with a yellow cream?
And then something passed between.

Now the terrible hushes
rasp out forbidden words
that sigh and heave.
He placed his hand upon the bud
and shook his brown and green
while licking slowly the full moist lips
and then something passed between.

She looked as deep
as she dared to
and asked, "how long is this day?"
"Long" he answered, "very long"
"and what of this night?" she pressed,
"Brief, twin of flesh,
brief as twenty two."
"What will I remember?"
"Nothing. Except what is agony to recall
and too haunting to escape."
You think you see all of now
but it is only a fragment
and that will define most of your past.

In your future I see now
a wish in your eyes
pushing that look into my face
longing to hear the halting whispers
where passion is time's bloodshot wink
where twenty two is forever
bathed in a yellow cream
all whipped into a lather
from a lamp lusting furnace.

In your touch a broken glass bottle
the razor shards that will pass for affection.

All the broken promises
that pass for what is between us
in silence and night dream
stuck fast
stiff and dry to youth's limb
in winter waiting for
the time that has no name
and you will slip your hand
into theirs
and go down the stairs.
While your other self stands astounded still
with a half opened mouth seeing at last
the door left ajar wide open wide.
Your own steps at the mercy of your feet
leading your heart's footprints down a fool's path
where your desire born of a wish granted
grew into a nightmare.

Because the dawn has this naked eye
to see between a twilight touch
and drenches morning in yellow cream.
Because the bloodshot brown and green
bled all down his face
and onto the sheets and into the streets.

Between the whispers the silence roars
as we pull together towards
the shallow shoals, the forgotten reefs
and those all too familiar rocky shores.
Because this heart has seen too many coats of paint
because the cellar is warm
between the sigh and heave.
Because the night is brief
where we fall to our heart's death in each other's eyes.
Because bitterly this once before I have seen

between the glow of whispers and grayness
any common rainbow hides.
All that passes between is
but a solitary flame of an extinguished dream
spoken in bloodshot whispers brown and green.

2/87

BAR WITHOUT MATCHES

Most of the boys in the can
don't really seem to belong
in there.
I see that if you take away a man's
beer, cigarettes, matches, woman,
children, drugs, money, wallet, streetclothes
and dress them in hospital pajamas with their
naked feet in flip flops they are just like
everybody else.

Such a wide collection of sad eyes.
The ones that really get to you are those who just
don't talk about it. Ever.
No hard luck stories, no ever-present alibis
just all of them sitting around the table
discussing the weather like just like plain folks.

Today they brought Graham into my classroom
under six-inch leg shackles and what appeared to be
a fairly new set of handcuffs.
He shuffled in and nodded his head affably in my
direction. I had the urge to ask, "Hey, what's up with
all the jewelry, Bud, you trying to make a fashion
statement?"
But this wasn't a George Raft movie.

I don't play around in here.
When I see him under double lock down, I don't wonder
what he did, I think more along the lines of,
"Gee, I'm glad at least the ankle and wrist bracelets are
metal, not those suck ass plastic ones they use these days
to bind a man off like he was a big black baggie of garbage.

I'd hate to have to wear a pair of those plastic bands.
It would be like drinking shots of Dewar's in little
disposable medicine Dixie cups.

I never did ask Graham about the bracelets.
It just wasn't any of my business, after all you
don't ask people on the street why they wear the kind
of shoes they do.

I walked over to turn down the Strauss on the CD player
and Graham looks up and says;

"Oh, leave it alone, it was so refreshing."

5/96

RECIPE FOR FORGOTTEN SPRING

Mainline Mundane Monday plopped out of the routine
bucket like a low level grayish-brown industrial toxic sludge.
Midday lunch hour clogged and gagged on itself. All the
gleaming fiberglass high-impact colored chariots paraded
up and down the avenues. The drivers and passengers
appeared already dead. Lifeless highly mobile donkey drones.
Trapped behind the wheel. Strapped in for dear life
squinting from behind smoke-tinted
bullet proof windshields.
Plainly put: the sad procession looked like a funeral
march and what the fuck were all those rolling Easter egg
colored penis shaped semi-miracle plastic cockroaches doing
stuffed with tender soft pudgy human meat and where were
they all going?

I was really amazed that no one was screaming.
You should have seen their blank expressionless faces.
I was looking for a hidden high sign.
A secret handshake. Twist of the decoder ring.
Some clue to tell me this was just a ghastly bad joke.
But it wasn't.
It was just modern life on a Monday.
It was just common citizens on an afflicted planet,
rolling along, bound by careers, groggy from comfort,
stupefied in uniformity.

Who could tell where they were all headed for:
Cholesterol screening at the Catholic Church.
Blood pressure/Stress test at the Union Hall.
Substance Abuse clinic at the Grange.
AA Meetings at the Oddfellows Auditorium.
Loyalty Oaths over at the Post Office.
Mandatory prayer hour at the minute man.
Physical jerks at the sound body/mind gym.

And me? Well, I was on my way to the cooking class that
I teach at the local detention center.
Today we were going to cover a brand new recipe.
It's called, "RECIPE FOR FORGOTTEN SPRING."
Perhaps you would like to have it for yourself.
Take out your pencils.
Here is the recipe for forgotten spring:
First; take the eyes and poke them out.
Any common skewer, knitting needle or ice pick
will do the job. (In a pinch steak knives are fine.)
Next you can use the same handy home kitchen tools
to puncture both ear drums.
Then, break your nose with either a meat tenderizer or
ballpeen hammer. Pack with duct tape and epoxy.

The reason for these basic preparations is that you
must properly prepare yourself in the kitchen so
all the Springtime budding, blossoming, and warming
sunlit air of May won't be a distraction to what you do next.
Now, Got any dreams? Take them and chop them up as
finely as possible, either by food processor or
with a stainless steel knife. (Watch them fingers,
remember you're blind.)
Just a thought at this point,
if you find you don't have any dreams of your own to
grind up, steal someone else's and puree theirs.

Take the ground up dreams and store them safely in the toilet.
Next cover the earth's crust evenly with as much
blacktop and concrete as you can. Slice and mince your
world into a gayly decorative pattern of strip malls,
shopping centers, miracle miles, fast food empires,
car dealerships, empty barren parking lots, radioactive
waste dumps. Really just about anything that looks as
ugly as it is useless.
Garnish with radish roses made of landfills.
Next pour into a measuring cup or IRS personal information
computer bank..people. All kinds. Colors, sizes, ages,
beliefs, income levels. Add the pure, the simple, the
mad, the indifferent. Pour the content of the measuring
cup into the blender of mundane modern routine and set
on blanderize for a lifetime.

At this point, all personality, imagination, individuality
and purpose should be a nice creamy grey scum, with an
aroma which is simply impossible to describe because of
the epoxy and duct tape stuffed up the nostrils of your
broken nose.

Fish the chopped up dreams out of the toilet and combine
with the creamy grey scum putting
them both into a two-inch
flat bottomed non-sticking baking pan. If you don't have
a pan of this sort, don't worry. Just flush those ground
up dreams right down the toilet and place the creamy grey
scum into positions of responsibility and spiritual guidance
(chances are no one will be able to tell the difference.)
Sprinkle the top of all this with nuclear missiles with hair
triggers and worn out safety systems, decaying space stations
and antiquated weather satellites, metal fatigued 737's
and for real global spice add a rogue asteroid. The finishing
touch comes with acres and acres of steel wire mesh for
that truly over-extended look.

Bake on fricassee at six million degrees for 90 or 100
years in the atmosphere until you're positive the ozone
layer is getting this nice even brown crust with huge
holes in it like arc-welded blocks of Eyehook Swiss cheese.
Flute the edges, slit the center and let explode all over
the inside of the oven or in this case, maybe just our
little corner of the milky way.

Chill thoroughly for the rest of eternity.

So now you can see how easy it is to bake this mess
when we have all forgotten spring. If you didn't get
a chance to write down this particular recipe and would
like to remember it, just look out your window next May.

So whether your favorite dish is a crispy nothingness
cobbler pudding, little flaky pastry or cool and tangy
dish of sherbet, remember; if the kitchen of your spring
is clean and tidy, pristinely unconcerned and you're so
proud of those nice long immaculate formica counters
of smugness, it's because you've got nothing cooking,
something instead is burning

Spring 88-98

DATE WITH NEVER

(For M.F.G.)

Everyone loved Chick Lorimer in our town.
Far off.
So we all love a wild girl keeping a hold
on a dream she wants.
Nobody knows now where Chick Lorimer went.

> From "Gone"
> Carl Sandburg
> Chicago Poems
> 1916

I was holding a box of strawberries
I was standing on the threshold
of a doorway to promise.
The car motor idles impatiently
eager to embark upon the journey.
As you reached to hand me the change
I clasped your hand in mine momentarily
and said, "goodbye, I'm going to miss you."
Your eyes widened a smile detonated bright.
In that instant a seed was planted wordlessly
in an Orient point farm field at Terry's stand.

The next time I saw you,
after the color of strawberries had faded,

after the sun in June's infinity had singed
away a portion of youth,
after years of strangers and miles,
we happened to fall together once more.

I found you sitting next to me riding in the white Plymouth.
I was still always leaving.
This time you were in the car with me.
Night had fallen.
We had a date
We had a date with never.
I can still hear your voice singing to me
at Duffy's bar later that night
to the Billy Joel on the jukebox.
I spent every dollar I had that evening.
You sang into my eyes.
The liquid of your voice
could have drowned me
right there.

Later we sat down at the end of Harbor River Road.
Mountains of midnight stacked up
in soft white cotton stairs stretching up to heaven.
The washing rhythm soaked the dark blue salt tides
and set the inlets to whispering.
A cream full moon shone:
bright as a phosphorescent silver dollar.
I remember thinking in awe: it was all like
a setting straight from a Capra movie.
Bedford Falls etched in New England mescaline.
You had the look of a very young Lee Remick.
Your skin shone.
Your eyes had the blue sparks of banked fires.

The only problem I wasn't him.

I wasn't Jimmy Stewart.
So when I admitted to you that I considered you
the kind of woman I would marry,
you quickly averted your eyes,
dropping them to the interior shadows and asked,
"Do you know where I can get some cocaine?"

Somehow I don't think that even Jimmy Stewart would
have an answer for that one.
But I do think you loved me, in some way,
for some reason that now sadly I will never have the
chance to make you explain to me.
I do regret your untimely passing.
I would have liked to see you just once
shaking with uncontrollable rage,
livid in hot furious tears,
being unreasonable in a public place.

I think we missed making a
couple of spectacular spectacles
both publicly and privately.

Now you will be 36 years old forever.
Frozen in your youth near the tail end of winter.
An infinity of waiting for spring right around the corner
waiting maybe for me with that curious squeak to your voice
that escaped when you grew excited or exasperated.
Once I dreamed you hid from me.
You hid in the blue tints
of the old theater's lobby mirrors.
Your expression one of a slight mocking astonishment
at just how brutal the life of those bound to the
earth and its rituals could be.

Wasn't it the last time we said goodbye

when all the sky was a shattered mirror.
A collapsing Cathedral showering stars
in glistening shards.
I took you in my arms and you became so very still.
Almost stiffening at my touch, looking at me
as if I wasn't wholly there.
I sensed this and began to release you.
And as I did this, you reached back for me,
clinging suddenly with your arms sealing about
my neck, locking tight.
Your face inches from mine,
just before you buried your face into my neck.
And you wouldn't let me pull away.

Did you whisper something then?
Something I can't clearly recall.
What was it in you that burned and shone?
So slightly moist and terrified it peeked out
at me so briefly from those translucent eyes.
Those quick eyes that darted away
always looking over my shoulder
always just a bit beyond me
always to someone else, somewhere else.
Was that the seed I planted in you?
Or merely the world you lusted for.

Did you ever see it?
Did you ever find it?

I can say these words to strangers now at the public
readings. I could look through old boxes for one of your
letters, just to see your slanting script and know your hand
once passed there.
Yet nothing would ever come back to me
like the sound of your voice

singing to me with the jukebox
at Duffy's bar that night.

Now I can hold you.
To my heart's content
right there on this page
in my own fashion
in a way I never
could quite hold you
in life.

3/95

KILL THE POET

(For B.H.)

I believe if you want something, you should ask for it.
If you want a drink, order up. (Politely)
If you want an explanation, make the inquiry. (Discreetly)
But if you ask for poetry and don't get any, our duty is
clear, just order a nice fresh beer and KILL THE POET.

Kill him. Simple solution isn't it. He's been asking for it.
He's just not delivering the GOODS. So don't be shy.
You're just not getting what you want. Why shouldn't
everybody get what they want?

Oh, the poor son of a bitch wants to SUFFER, right?
Why not put him out of his misery. Settle his hash. Shoot him.
Administer a good sound public beating. You'll be
glad you did and your friends will thank you. And as for
the poet...he'll probably WRITE about it. Poor dopey bastard
NEEDS the INSPIRATION.
From what we can gather from his blather,
nothing quite moves him like his own suffering.
So do him a favor. Do yourself a favor. In fact do ALL of
us a favor, do it right now.

Ask to be told by one of these self-absorbed petty pundits
why the current the state of the arts is the friggin
ME club with the golden rule; don't you tell me the truth

about my stuff and I won't tell you the truth about how
fucking lame your crap is. Remember our job is not art.
Our use of the grant money is to
PROMOTE AND PERPETUATE the HOAX of our "talent"
and the "myth" of our expression's worth.

So just go and make a "retro" selection from one of the
four major beatnik food groups: alcohol, caffeine, tobacco,
and soup. Then take a deep breath, grab a handful of
the night air and walk up to the poet and shake it in
his face and say, "here you go, you old sorry-assed
literary wizard, you missed all this, didn't you.
You were so busy showing off with your carefully chosen
preoccupied lexicon, making certain you assaulted our
senses with perfectly malformed poignant bullshit
that you missed the point.

YOU'RE JUST NOT SAYING ANYTHING ANYONE
WANTS, NEEDS, OR SHOULD HAVE TO HEAR!

Sure, your heart is like a peeled grape rolled in salt.
Sure, the magic wonder of your houseplant at sunset is
...is...BREATHTAKING.
Yes I know as a child you were beaten at dawn by vampires
with nunchucks. You are so MISUNDERSTOOD.
(Good thing too, if anyone could figure your ass out,
the jig would be up on the "Poor poet in the wilderness
routine.")

Want a small piece of advice?
No, of course not.
I'm advising you to SHADDUP, already.
Cease and desist the whining and pleading, imploring
and apologizing, constructing those little unicorn
bridges in the air,

WE'VE TAKEN A STRAW POLL AND WE
ARE ABOUT TO HANG YOU FROM IT. (at sunset)
Why don't you start delivering something.
Hell, pizza would be a good start. What the hell?!?
At least we could eat that! Look we could SHARE!

Don't you know anything good?
Like Clark Gable was known to stop off in the desert
and at some lost beat greasy diner, order steak and eggs
and fuck any damn waitress he liked.
Ty Cobb once stabbed a thief who tried to rob him in
an alleyway fight and was cut up himself pretty good.
He slapped a strip of adhesive tape bandage over the
belly gash and went out the next day against the pirates
and went three for three. (Two doubles amd a triple,
you can look that up)
No, you don't know any of that stuff and the problem is you
could give a rat's ass what your audience might want.
Give us stories, huge funny lies, images that burn, sing,
soar or amaze.
ANYTHING except SANCTIMONY and SEMANTICS.

So, how about that? Mr. Edgar Alan dude.
You've been warned.
We are onto you. Don't push your poetic license or we
will stamp a 666 across your Dewars and donkey dog ticket.
Don't make us kill the poet.

Poets should try to keep the moment alive.
Not beat the damn thing to death.
Perhaps suspend precious time artfully,
not hang it by the neck till dead by strangulation.
Don't take the word execution so literally.

Some night really look at the faces of those sitting
through one of your COMMAND Performances.
Please take note. Does the audience appear to be
 SUFFOCATING like snagged catfish gasping for AIR at
your feet, on the bottom of the boat.
YOU need to give us something we can breathe.
Yes, we are no match for you. Such LITTLE fish.
Fine. Throw us back in. It's a BIG ocean.
Perhaps it's all a simple matter of "being in one's
own element."
Is it too much to hope for that you could decide to immerse
us in something a little deeper than that dinky plastic
pail of bitter bile and bay water backwash?

You may be amazed by this,
but there really are those who
love poetry, love poets. They know what's good. They don't
need you to DEFINE it for THEM.

Maybe, just maybe it could be that the BEST poetry doesn't
need poets or words or workshops. Could it be that what is
communicated transcends composition because it tends to
exist, already alive and composed, in the human spirit,
in the natural elements.

LET ME REFRESH YOUR MEMORY. That would be
EARTH, WIND, AIR and FIRE.
NOT NARCISSISM, MASTURBATION, SOPHISM and
        INTELLECTUAL SNOBBERY
(not to mention the deconstructional genderizing of the
group sexual dynamics on Gilligan's Island)

The poets who are loved, not dreaded are the ones who know

that they are merely the messengers, the conductors, the
conduits through which flow, escape, dance,
swing the graceful or distasteful aspects of human nature.
Those poets who, at least
TRY to express that honestly. They make an EFFORT to
include everyone. To reflect clearly what it is TO BE
ALIVE with great joy or great pain. They say, THIS is just
not MINE, it is YOURS too, in a fashion that's undeniable.

So will you forgive me that you and your anesthetized
entourage sipping expresso striking attitudes concerned
with excluding the common multitudes who...just don't
appreciate our genius leaves me cold.
Take your stale little clique,
your minor league literary elitism,
your stuck-on-yourself demeanor that states..
WE KNOW...you don't. WE ARE....you aren't.
WE COUNT...you don't and GET LOST.

So you see we really don't want to kill you.
We NEED all the POET'S POEMS we can find in our lives.
Make yourself useful there, Mr. and Mrs. Edgar Alan dude,
  write something that is alive. Something we can share.
Heal, bless, forgive, fertilize, make us remember, help
us understand this wild one shot at life.
You want to help mankind?
Tell funnier jokes in your poems, or at least you could
show up with that pizza, some sandwiches of reality,
maybe a little fresh air, ideas, perspective, sentiments.
How about coat pockets full of surprises, gifts, drinks
on the house!

The WORD is OUT on you.

STOP it with the endless mouthfuls of microwavable
metaphorical meatus munching milk toast.
You can't go on being some kind of goddamn parallel
universe Santa Claus with a bag full of prose coal,
because everybody has been BAD again this year.

We are TRYING to be GOOD.
After all, we haven't KILLED the POET.
Yet.

88/98

YOU BE THE AUDIENCE

You be the audience
you be the judge.
Just do what we do best here in America:
sit and watch...hide and hate...judge and bitch.
You be the audience.
It's time we talked.
It's time we started to try and understand
just what it is we expect
from a lifetime of passive grey glue cable watching.

You be the audience;
but I'm not the poet.
That's just another name or label.
A trade mark like an OLDS CUTLASS SUPREME
or long range surface to air missiles
or Demi Moore or acceptable levels of dioxin
or a quest for your personal best home computer
fitted with E-Mail condoms equipped with a
reservoir tip for brainstorms.

You be the audience;
I don't have a part color video intercut with slow
motion black and white grainy footage of desire laden
lips that pout and sneer or drool over product image.
No back beat. No window vibrating bass lines.
No Freudian titillation synthesizers.
No samples of misogynist home-boys bawling at 5 a.m. for
another line of blow. Listening to this won't increase your

positive cash flow or make your investment sense
grow or provide for you
a clue as to what you are supposed to reap from a lifetime
of consumption and passivity.

I am not motherfucking A.J. SQUARED away puppet model
poet faking it in some lame dick Docker's commercial.
You can't market poetry
like Fruit n' Fiber Nuttin Honey.

You be the audience.
But haven't you always?
From pampered pussed hot house flowers grown in the
depleted middle class soil of your parents' living room
to confused smug fashioned faced soap opera stars.
You've watched and watched and watched.

You're experts at watching orchestrated reality from a
safe distance.
You exist in Michelob nights and Maxwell House mornings
where you're fucked softly by either tubes of toothpaste
or breath mints.
After all;
you are the audience.

You are so smart, beautiful, graceful, sophisticated.
Your blind desire for pure useless crap
drives our cultural marketplace.
And what's our collective payoff?
Pink Penis Max Factor glossy, creamy bullets
Christian Dior dildos fashioned out of pepperoni and denim
You be the audience.
Silent arrested development mouths puckered lips smeared
in boiled whale grease substitute.
You hear this and react in stray coughs, limited attention

spans, and bewildered shock thinking,
what can this be?
Imitation, copyright infringement or intimidation.

You be the audience.
You think like canceled programming:
syndicated idiots in the heat of the night, wondering
who's the boss or is it Charles in Charge?
You're thirty something or golden girls puzzling over the
passing of your wonder years. Just another world where
your two dads divorce to lust after the young and the
restless. Your current affair ends up in night court
just another version of beauty and the beast meets
Miami vice to end up staying home on a Saturday night
with Jake and the fatman watching all of Freddie's
nightmares.

You be the audience.
I know what you know.
We see each other all the time
and decide hard fast things about each other,
without a single shred of fact to base them on.
Just good old fashioned modern American class consciousness
 and snobbery anchored firmly in fear and hate.
We don't like what we don't know.
And we don't seem to want
to know much of anything.

You be the audience
but you don't want poetry.
You want power, money and self-important careers that you
can hold over each other's head. You want Cadavers with rich
Corinthian leather. You want recognition, accolades for
being useless self absorbed guest stars in your own
miserable miniature mini-series all about YOU.

You want deferments that absolve you of any
responsibility, accountability or moral liability.
This is a shame too.
Because there is poetry out there.
It's in the street, in the kitchen, waiting for you
out in the back yard, on the train, down at the
water front. In a hundred places you would never think
to look because the act requires effort and imagination.

You don't think in poetry.
You associate poetry with Hallmark, literacy workshops,
trite broken heart sentiment
You'll find no poetry in your paycheck
No poetry in your personal programmable laser disc man
No poetry on tabloid inquisitional television
No poetry washing your hands of life every day
No poetry there. Period.
No poetry in carefully cultivating an attitude that common
people are not priceless treasures and anybody else is
just another asshole without the benefit of your
personal endorsement and benediction.

You be the audience.
But don't you wonder for how much longer?
What do you think maintains some semblance of sanity,
humanity and normalcy to try and hold the world together.
If you don't.
How long do you expect this country, this culture, this
world to spin and revolve around you,
exist solely for your personal convenience.
What kind of temper tantrum would you throw
if there was a limited exchange nuclear war?
Just think. What a hassle it would be trying to shop
during the food riots. Wouldn't the disappearance of
flushing toilets be inconvenient?

What you mean the VCR doesn't work without electricity?
What you mean the microwave doesn't work ...what about my
hot pockets?

What do you mean there's no more electricity?
No answering machines, E-mail tag, cell phone fun.
No more NiMo, No more Milk Duds, Lean Cuisine,
What's that about my Amanda Six-tier comfort zone
refrigerator's ice-maker?
I wanted that on the rocks!!!
What do you mean no more cozy warm snug narcotic
American split-level suburban base-board heated
reality!!!!

What do you mean my world has become a black, arctic
frost bowl of nuclear winter in 36 hours?

I was in the audience. I said I care about poetry.
Of course I had very little of it in my life. I treated
people in my world like disposable, faceless,
non-entities. I never stood for anything. Never tried to
understand anything. Never even thought of trying to make
things in general any better.
I just hid and consumed.
Sat and watched.
Judged and hated.
Hey, look.........I had "stuff" to do.
You be the audience
But do you ever wonder
for how long?

Spring 87

HOW TO FIND AN AFTERNOON BAR

(For B.P.)

Take late October
sniff the wind on the corner.
See Autumn's color and feel grey and small.

Notice at the curb
stiff windshield faces,
a bit worse off
for all the routine.
They wouldn't run you over.
On purpose.

Check the four P.M. light.
Sniff the wind on that corner.
Take late October
right where she stands.

Walk in.
Take a good fast look around.
Got it?
You'll catch the bartender's eye
(if you look ready)
NEVER CALL OR YELL.
Have your money out.
During your first transaction

you should be gravely polite.

Then akimbo the elbows
and watch the door and take a sip.
Wonder openly with your mouth shut.
More polite indifference.
Have your money ready.
Have a newspaper.
Spread it out like a bib.
MIND YOUR BUSINESS.
Be preoccupied
with the routine.

Drink. Light up, flick, drink, crush out.
(Repeat as necessary)
Sink your neck a little deeper
into your haunches.

Laugh.....when they laugh.

Grow serious.....when they grow serious.
Never whine. Stammer or sulk.
Never hit three bars before five.

Somebody expecting you for supper?
Keep that in mind.
Because when it's cold
it's gone.

Then it's leftovers for you
and a reheated anything stinks.

Don't lecture fools
or comment on the obvious,
(keep your two cents in your pocket).

Be patient.
Know if you push it
long enough,
a ghost will eventually show up.
Something.
Even if they don't know it.
Even if you don't know it.
Do you really want to know
if they ever knew it or not.

Remember elation
can be a by product of three beers
and despair can follow on the heels of four.

Don't answer pay phones.
Remember, you're not here.
But be disappointed when it's not for you.

Avoid pontification.
Know when to grin.
Know when to narrow the eyes.
Know when it's time to blow.

Leave the chips for your shoulder out in the street.
Hard faces and gestures are their own reward.
If you need a map or excuse
cut it short.

If the place is unfriendly
be dignified and diplomatic.
If it's sullen and tense
be angelic and menacing.
Nod....when they nod.
Stare....at what they stare at.

Think of other afternoons
other soft soaks
in a bar near a pier.
Think of all the lost pals
 who are exiled elsewhere.

Take the elevator down
to the basement in your heart
where all those memories are stored
in brown cardboard boxes.
Think mildew.

Lament other bartenders past.
Who knew you.
Knew your routine.
And were tolerant
to the point of kindness.
All the past bartenders
who always fixed you up
when the day had all but broken.

Touch your finger
to the side of your forehead
take the thumb and fingerprint the temple
and leave it in their tip.

Sniff the air.
Take October.

Fall 87

HAVEN FOR HAYES

I am the night watchman in the garden of ghosts.
I keep the events that are passed over.
I know the tones of forgotten poems.
I remember what you long to forget.

One day you will know my prison
where the bars are temples of hope and despair
bathed in deep red low lights that
shine and shimmer to illuminate a forgotten lineage
of true blue blood.

I see your round eye when I enter the room.
The naked plain disgust on your face.
I marvel at that cruel mocking smirk.
This I have clearly earned
by my words, my face,
the simple fact of my presence.
The nerve. the nerve.
Why....the very idea.

Your spirit is an out of tune piano
that no one has ever touched the right keys
in a sequence that could move you
beyond yourself.

Did anybody ever get any music out of you anyway?

I will make this right.
I am the idiot apparition of Paderewski
with a beat up suitcase of stolen
forbidden sheet music.
I am a tone deaf train roaring down the main line
only to be derailed by a gingham blouse
draped across the track bed.

I am one of the original New York Mets,
cut from the squad on Christmas Eve at the Polo Grounds.
I still have the infield grit in my teeth.
Stengel once snarled,
"Good boy...though I never could understand a word he said,
but he was good for a laugh or grounder in the adam's
apple. It was a shame, he never could figure out if he
should throw the screw ball or be a screw ball."

The Hall of Fame
or was that the shack of obscurity
was always firmly beyond my reach.

I sing into the face
of the moron smugness.
I have been through the mill
I have endured daily beating from strange hands
for vague reasons.
Still I wish for you
one solid blind surprise
that could obliterate
your knack for perpetual disappointment.
What of that general disenchantment you harbor
so deeply in a dark secret swallow inlet
where only little ships are allowed brief mooring.

I was born in the Sound.

Blue, salty and more than slightly polluted.
I know how to flow and flush
and will never back up into the bowl
for your fouled pipes.

I am the unpleasant reminder.
I have done the Bataan Death March of Education.
I am permanently certified in this State.
I teach and educate your children.

I am Lee Marvin as drunken gunslinger.
I will sober up just enough to shoot your lights out.

I have fucked your daughters
and no it wasn't safe sex.
It was all very dangerous and expensive.
We left each other in ruins and shambles.
My message escaped beyond to live and thrive
despite the small minded spermicide and
ill fitted diaphragms of betrayal.
One diminutive spark of prose survived
to bring to life a common act.

I am the Mister Roberts of Poetry.
Assigned, resigned to be lost on
some trivial supply ship sailing between
tedium and toil.

And don't I wish for my Ensign Pulver
to be at my elbow.
I have a picture of you
framed over my bunk.
I want to remember the face
that sent me here.

And don't I want into the war.
The war between your ears.
I want you to read between the lines
of my apocalypse by apoplexy.
I want you to know if given the chance,
"I'll build a house of arrogance
a most peculiar inn
with only room for vanquished folk
with proud and titled chin!"

1/92

JULY 90

At last summer kissed once a night like this
all with intentions of attention
we show because we hope and desire
under the thick humming black wire
full of gossip and sure things gone to seed
in this blackness full of watchful eyes banking on another's
misfortune and at least one solid prefabricated lie
to assure us that all this is another dismissal epistle from
a damaged agnostic beatnik prophet with an axe to grind.
A score card to fill out. A diamond to run around.
In short, this is a fan letter to a corporate conglomerate
with a heart of actual human being, who has the nerve to
think about life before Robo Cop nights and sound bite dawns
that are always oddly on line.
Here insist upon the smell of Noxzema and Ammens Original
Scent let loose upon the skin this night when the heart has
only this to say for itself the sound of the neighbors in the
next yard over pitching horse shoes with a clink and a clink
and dull clank. There was a distant roar of traffic and the
sharp faint pinpoints of carnivorous vampiric fire flies
signaling to a lover to come to dinner. Guess who's on the
menu tonight.

My little boy comes in the living room singing.
"My daddy's gone chemical, I heard it on TBS
Turner knows. He got a word of knowledge from Pat.
He knows what kind of deep trouble my old man is in.
They can put Trump on a tight budget, but my dad spends our

money like he was some soft spoken white trash middle age
medium roller on holiday at the black jack table.
You sit there like a kind of bland half ass jury with
twelve angry men gagging in the corner of the court room.
The judge a bitter dissolute ex-dreamer who's beyond all
that horse shit now. You can watch his face and that cruel
states, pal, you've just crapped out in front
of all of us good kind Christian folk. We just knew it was
a matter of time till you would end up down here.
Ranting and babbling and qualifying at the remarkable
indifference in the daylight hours of this time gone
numb and judgmental in the interest of justice.
The news of nightfall on the express track with the
signal lights all frozen open on dead eye green.
This time it would be to serve and protect one's own
little set of misconstructions. Tight assed little things.
To paraphrase Vonnegut, Our heads are encased in steel spheres
and there is only one eyehole through which we got to
look through six feet of pipe, while we are strapped to a
steel lattice which is bolted to a flatcar on rails, and
there was no way we could turn the head or touch the pipe.
To top this off you don't even know you're on the flat car
going ninety toward a discontinued sideline. In fact you don't
think day to day anything peculiar about the situation.
"Sometimes the flatcar creeps, sometimes it goes like a
bat outta hell, then jerks to an abrupt standstill. Uphill,
downhill around curves, along straightaways.
Whatever you poorbastards see through that pipe,
you shake your heads a little and sigh
"That's Life."

July 90

A GOOD STORY

(For L.)

It was a bitterly cold night. They were in bed together.
They were sober enough to talk to each other. Usually they
stumbled home drunk as lobotomized ducks, tore off each
other's clothes, till there was this small mound of
multicolored fabric next to the bed. Then they would make
love till one of them passed out. This seldom disturbed
or discouraged the other. At times they failed to notice.
But tonight was different. She was wide awake. He was
reading. The bed was like a boat bobbing warmly on winter seas.
She said, "Tell me a story."
Not looking up from his book, he said, "Nah."
"C'mon" she said, "you used to tell me stories all the time."
"That was different," he said,
"I was trying to get you into bed."
"Well," she said, "if you want to keep me here, you
better come up with one fast."
He thought for a minute.
"O.K." he said, "Once upon a time I was on this bus
going from coast to coat for 99 dollars back east for
Christmas. I sat in the only seat left all the way in
the back of the bus. There was this girl sitting in
front of me with red hair and freckles. She was an
artist. She was sitting with these big, mean looking
black guys. They had one thing in their mind. She was
being real friendly and nice and by the time we hit the

mountains of Idaho at two in the morning, after the
endless reefers, bottles of cheap champagne and boxes
of Banquet chicken, they started to get rather ugly and
began molesting the lady artist and I stood and...."

"Yeah, I know that one," she said, "Then you saved
her from the barbarians and you sat with her and by
Cleveland, you were necking with her. I still don't
believe it. I know that story. C'mon... tell me a good
story."

"O.K." he said, "Once upon a time I was working as a
night orderly for the Burger King of Geriatrics and that
night we were short-handed, as usual, and I was breaking in
this new guy on the job who looked like a cross between
Dirty Harry and a big wolf. I had told him to go down the
other end of the hallway and work his way up towards me.
As I was strapping this crazy old man into bed for the
night, I heard this scream from down near the nurse's
station. I ran to the room where he was and there was this
patient we called "Willard" because he only had one tooth
and looked a lot like a scruffy rat, standing barefoot in
a pool of his own blood. He had his catheter, all yanked
out, with the ball still inflated and his other hand
was holding his........"

"NO," she groaned, "That's GROSS! I don't want to hear
about that again. What a gruesome story, I've heard you
harp on that place before, yeah, I know you're a regular
saint. C'mon....tell me a good story...."

"O.K." he said, " Once upon a time I lived in this two
story walk up matchstick fire trap, that was most certainly
condemned out on the waterfront. My roommate and I used to
pay fifty bucks a month to the guy downstairs who ran a

combination vacuum cleaner/porno book store. One day he
just disappeared. We didn't know who to pay. So we forgot
about it and lived there for free.

This apartment was the size of an empty aircraft carrier.
It was so much empty space that it echoed when you talked.
There was this one big picture window. It was the size of
the entire front wall. The view opened up to overlook the
bay, the islands in the distance, the factory that made
toilet paper at four in the morning, the railroad yards,
and the parking lot of this bar called The Blue Dolphin.
There wasn't any heat in this apartment, and since it was
only November, we could survive with space heaters in
our bedrooms. We would wait for the sun to shine into the
living room through the huge picture window and kind of
warm up the place a little. Then we would sit on that battered
couch in the sunlight, getting as stoned as stunned flies,
listen to ENO and watch the bums down in the street walk
up and down the sidewalk below on their way to the mission.

The best part was the hallway where the stairs leading up to
the second floor where we lived. There was this one long
stairwell where some old acid head or nut or somebody had the
notion to rip up this sheet music book of popular
songs from the sixties. This person had taken some time
to plaster the wall with the musical scores, at odd angles
up and down the staircase all about the crumbling plaster
and peeling wall paper. There were some great songs like:
AUTUMN LEAVES, HONEY, TO SIR WITH LOVE,
WIPE OUT, WHIPPED CREAM, SIDEWALKS OF NY,
JAVA, LAZY DAY, PLEASE LOVE ME FOREVER,
I DON'T WANT TO SET THE WORLD ON FIRE,
COTTON CANDY, WALK....DON'T RUN, NEVER ON
A SUNDAY, I LEFT MY HEART IN SAN FRANCISCO,
HARPER VALLEY PTA, TURNAROUND LOOK AT ME,

ALFIE, SOMETHING STUPID, WHERE HAVE ALL THE
FLOWERS GONE, CITY OF NEW ORLEANS,
SEPTEMBER SONG, LIKE A ROLLING STONE.

It was the best staircase in the world. But you could
tell it wouldn't last. Every day more and more music had
fallen off the walls and littered the steps.

So for the time being I would climb the musical staircase
every morning after work. I would slowly take it step
by step. Stopping to turn my head and hum or sing a few
bars of whatever song was on eye level. This went on
for about two months.

Then one day I was lying on the mattress on my
bedroom floor and the door flew open and there was this
well heeled real estate lady with a big Indian in a
purple fringed jacket and she wanted to know what we
were doing in there.

And I said, "singing and freezing, most of the time."
But that was it. We were asked to vacate the premises.
And we did without argument after that we were...."

She was half asleep mumbling into the pillow,
"no....no...no...tell me a good story... a good story."
"So you want a good story...huh?" he whispered,
"O.K. but you're not going to hear it. Or believe it.
Or like it."

Once upon a time in the not so distant future,
you won't love me anymore.
You'll wonder what it was that you ever saw in me.
You'll sneak into town some night and fuck a local
joker behind my back.
You'll run out on me and go back to your mother

You'll tell all your friends what a loser I was
and what a mistake we were...
Soon you'll love somebody else, just like you did me.
You'll tell funny stories
about my foolishness and your foolishness for ever
putting up with it all.
You'll never believe how cruel it will all get.
And you'll have to have the abortion
because you don't want to have the baby.
You'll forget all about this.
And you'll grow older
and I'll grow older
and the time will pass
and you will wonder
what it is that I wonder
when I think about all this.
And we both will wonder how this moment here in this
bed tonight ever existed in time.
You'll see a face in a newspaper and it will remind
you of something.
And I'll see this woman on a Soap opera
and turn the channel.
But the face of the memory in the touch of what we
did in each other's hearts will never completely go
away. No matter how many years pass and whose arms we
ended up in.
And what was our story, will just become
another story that happened to a lot of people.

He turned to her. She was snoring softly. Her hair a
root beer halo spread over the pillow like a carpet of
down. She snuggled deeper and mumbled something.
He kissed her cheek and put out the light.
And the bedroom was warm, peaceful and quiet.

The street light came into the window softly setting
still like a ghost.
He fell asleep watching that light until I was curled up
in a ball on the floor in the palm of the ghost's hand.

And he heard a voice say, "tell me a story..
Tell me a good story."

1/85

THE DRIFT

Toward the middle of the decade
he found he could not listen to anything
that was tuned in properly.
Cable channels had a life span of twenty seconds
much less in reality.
The radio was dead in his ears.
Voices were at least tolerable.
Short Wave band 2 had a crisp pair of young commentators
speaking back and forth in
German intermixed with sentimental
Hebrew and gypsy laments
acting as musical history lesson
as retold by a drunken jukebox making a fool out of himself
just for old times sake.

Yes, it was a jumble.
But it was home.

                                                        11/93

MARCH ASSIGNMENT:

Waiting for the games to begin
Vaguely wishing for release
from my own watchful eyes
release into the ears
what breaks for
icy doors, the icy looks
an icy appraisal
icy hopes
warmed by the booze
and the hot water
steamy spiral into the sink slipping
down drain's promise
holding the line within a dime
to hold the tender flesh swollen with youth
that has no need to remember
beyond the angle of a closing door
time now to speak to the pale guardians
of a lot of time to kill
and nothing to be.

90

DROWNING THE FIN

(For J.Y.)

We exchanged beaten faces
in a slow moving check out lane
in the market place on a Monday night.
You in your aisle.
I in mine.
No hint of the wild years between,
not one knowing glance,
just two men at the doorstep
of middle age looking at
each other's archway fading to obscurity.

That set of wounded eyes.
The big let down of an ordinary world
where you are on your way home
and I'm going the other direction.
The usual thing
I'm going to drown a fin.
And think
after three days of bright sunshine
in this grey place
that left no one warmed
and now as the soft wisps
of snow encroach
I wonder where
Castor and Pollux are tonight.

2/94

LOST DREAMSONG

(For J.B.)

Shepherd Sherbet
sang the olive skinned girl
in the bone ghost gingham dress
lacing the air with a vapor glare
the classroom was a series of stage flats
a diorama in crucible.
He sat waiting for the coming night
to mercifully suck the light out of the street
and cast the cartoon into shadows so that they could all be
    married with symptoms.

"All this blandishment" bleated the omnivorous chorus
perched on the burgundy ottoman
"We trust the relevancy of your lunacy
either laundry or lubber or loyalist long shot
you were the favorite dark horse
with clean hooves, so come to me
and bring those crocodiles
in your head."

"Will they cry?"
Whimpered the treadmill.
"Yas dey tragic as can be all right."
Lucky fer you, there is such a thing as second winds
stoicism and first light.

                                      6/90

DROWN

Back in the red booth
with a tall green bottle of beer
he sat out the last days of the year.
It was a quiet Sunday night before New Years Eve.
The bar was nearly empty. The floor was covered with
Calendar pages. He listened to the fan over the door.
He passed time as it passed him. It was easy. In fact
he had found it even worked the other way. Time could pass
him as he passed it. It was fine. On the mounted television,
Toma was giving some straight talk to teens about mixed
drinks. A drunk at the bar remarked, "He's loaded, I can tell,
look at the way his eyes water, musta had a fifth of Gin
before he came on." Then the man slammed his glass down on
the bar and some ice escaped. It sat there, on the slow melt.
It was fine. Now time was passing them all together.
He thought about the great hot greasy slices of pizza around
the corner. Just waiting. For him. To order. All that yellow and
white and red ready to make your mouth proud. He liked to
think about it all as much as he did eating it all. But later.
Now he was contented to watch the TV some more. Sally
worked the bar. Pretty good too. Heavy set, perpetually tired
looking Armenian woman in her fifties, no bullshit, not a
lump, strong willed, saloon smart, she didn't have much to
say as a rule, could size you up pretty quick, two kinds,
she thought, the players and the buyers.
She was polite enough, but cause any trouble
and she would use the laser on you in
a wink of Syndication waiver rights.

It was pretty quiet now, though.
Slow eight ball drown the round robin, down at the other end.
Somebody guarded the pay phone making seven bucks an hour.
If it rings he says,
"No, they didn't slice his tongue yet...yeah the tip I think."
"No... I don't know what they're gonna use... Maybe the lid of
a can of tuna...shouldn't make much difference...he'll sing.
Pretty quick. And then we're gonna make him eat that fuckin
pizza he keeps dreaming about."
He took a swig of beer. Then he got up to take a leak in the
back. His life back then, it was grand.

March 1990

TRIBUTE

He was struggling not to wake up at dawn.

He was dreaming about being in the desert and falling down in agony with his mouth open and choking on a throat full of sand. His tongue felt like a breaded baby veal patty that was starting to plug his wind pipe. When at last, in the pale light he was fully awake, he discovered that he had the blanket stuffed half way down his throat and his tongue was covered with fabric hairs. He started to gag and retch, knocking over the three-quarters of flat, warm beer in the bottle set on top of the small black and white television into the bed sheets. Screaming obscenities, he bolted up and immediately a bolt of pain shot through his head. It was like he had been picked off by a sniper with a high-powered scope from a distant roof top. Blacking out, he dropped like a sack of wet, rotten potatoes back down to the soggy bed clothes.

Approximately twenty-five minutes later, he came to again. "This time," he thought, "I'm going to take it slow." The light in the room was a good deal brighter. Hangovers like these on bright sunny days were a major league test of sanity and endurance. He pulled the blanket over his head. Something felt damp. Fearing the worse, he decided not to wonder any further. "Maybe I can fall asleep like this for the rest of the day," he reasoned. However the fart leaked so slowly, with an innocent hiss of escaping venom that the deadly ensuing atmosphere compelled him to whip off the covers and gasp at the somewhat fresher air in the room. This made him dizzy. Following on the heels of a roller coasting wave of nausea, he had to very quickly ascertain whether or not he'd make the bathroom in time. Bounding off the bed and staggering to fight for balance like he was dealing with the rules of gravity on another planet, he tripped, lurched forward and solidly smacked his head against the door knob.

Regaining consciousness this time, he had no idea how long he had been out. Still the journey to the bathroom was of the utmost urgency. Blinded by brilliant shafts of sunlight in the living room, he made the bowl with seconds to spare. If he hadn't been bare bottomed, it wouldn't have been a contest. The beer shit broke like a tidal wave of hot, stinking tourist faces oooohing and aaaahing at Niagara Falls. Relief was immediate, however temporary. The sheer force of the act of defecation set off a chain reaction in an equally impressive fire hydrant force torrent that exploded out his other end.

When at last he managed to clean up himself and the bathroom's walls and floor to at least the degree of the monkey house at the zoo in Central Park, he lurched back towards the salvation of the bed to pass out and hopefully die in.

Leaning up against the bedroom door jamb, he stood stunned and weaving, puzzled at what he was seeing. Over on the other side of the battered bed, wrapped in the soaked sheets, was a form of some considerable size topped off with a wild black nest of curly abundance. It shifted slightly. He put both hands up to his face and gasped, "Who the hell is that?"

Good Night Hank. Good Night Frank. Good Night Jack.

All about the midnight campfire the mutant vacuum cleaner moved to an intoxicating gypsy melody as mysterious floating castanets snapped out a pulsating rhythm. The ghost musicians of the infinity orchestra swung into the theme of the overture. Bassoons, base clarinets, trumpets, trombones glistened and shimmered in the pale autumnal moon light. One by one they filed into the midnight campsite: Cleetus Awreetus-awreetus, Uncle Meat, Ruben and the Jets and Suzy Cream cheese while flesh ripping weasels and prancing hot rats raced and cavorted in the dancing shadows from the open pit fire alive with licking sky orange and yellow tongues.

Edgar Varese makes the grand entrance and steps up to the podium and picks up the conductor's baton.

Tapping it twice on the music stand a hush falls over the assembled throng.

From stage left, a tall thin dark man with a guitar slung over his shoulder like an enchanted axe lopes towards his position amongst the musicians.

As he plugs in, there is a burst of electric static bolts in short circuited current as the arc of blinding white sound leaping in curve of a scimitar slices flowing energy driven in bending notes like a mad stampede of Pigmy Ponies and wild donkeys escaping out of the stacked rows of amplifiers. As the return of the son of Monster Magnet breaks into the Ritual Dance of the Child-killer, the audience starts to chant, "Help I'm a Rock".

The ecstatic flood of cacophony forced into copulation with euphonious fantasia opens the ear doors to other worlds of sound and sensation. The tall skinny guy with droopy thin black mustache cracks a blue bull whip of shining scintillation in animal rhythm given syncopation. His fingers a blur that halt suddenly. The silence is deafening. As the orchestra prepares for the second movement the patrols of the Brain Police descend on the campsite in droves. Arrests are ordered. Instruments confiscated. The officer in charge begins a long threatening speech, making accusations of atrocities perpetrated on order, harmony, decency, and good honest folks. His wrath is directed especially toward the dark guitarist. "YOU", he bellows with the blue veins bulging like swollen extension cords on the crown of his shaved skull, "ARE RESPONSIBLE FOR ALL THIS MADNESS AND UGLINESS AND DEPRAVITY. YOUR PERVERSION HAS INFECTED GENERATION AFTER GENERATION WITH YOUR VILE TWISTED OUTLOOK. HOW DARE YOU POISON THE AIRWAVES WITH THIS SATANIC COMPOSITION THAT YOU POUR INTO THE HEAVENS!!!!!!

Calmly putting his instrument back in the case, the tall thin man in the Mr. Green Jeans overalls and hanging strands of long black curls says, "Hey, stop it, you'll hurt your throat."

Good Night Hank. Good night Frank. Good Night Jack.

It was forever Saturday December and it was raining in Midtown and I crawled up on the mushroomed steel stool with the cyclops eye of plastic marbled white and green or blue or red Naugahyde bowling ball patterns stamped all over the seat.

My feet dangled about eight full inches from the raised foot rest step as I perched the elbows there on a wonderful cool smooth linoleum counter world. I could spin fully around once, twice looking up at him and smile.

Then the man dressed in the working whites, drying his hands on the towel tucked into his pants, who had shaved himself pretty badly and was red scabbed Nick with the Joe Torre perpetual five o'clock shadow who when he looked at you all innocent wide eyes seemed to grin in spite of himself. He handed the huge plastic coated menus to you and your father and turned to walk away only to return seconds later with a glass that was full of a million perfectly packed pieces of diamonds and bubbles with a straw stuck in the middle of it. And you asked him, "hey, what's this?" And he threw over his shoulder, "S'matter kid, never had a 7up?" And your heart leapt because you never had before and knew this was only the beginning. And you were just back from confession at St. Francis or fresh off the Santa Claus special excursion train or outside of a newly born turnpike when she whispered to you, "Now you can have anything you want, honey, just remember I want you to finish it all."

You were then allowed to order from the menu by yourself and the big man in white behind the counter standing in front of the stacked cups and the steaming pots and the sizzling grills and hissing fans, while overhead the bright flourescent lights buzzed and he actually listened to what you said and he wrote it all down.

And then you said, "thank you."
And there were more smiles all around.

You looked up at your father, young and sleek, with David Nivin's mustache holding his cup of coffee and freshly lit cigarette and asked, "Hey after lunch can we go to see Radio city?" And the answer was yes. It was almost always yes. He looked down at you and your eyes locked in an endless joy of trust and companionship that passed wordlessly between hearts forever in time and memory.

The great plate glass window in the front of the coffee shop steamed at the corners while the world was alive in deadly chaos out there on the sad sidewalk earth. But, from where you sat then there was a jeweled anchor in her eyes to protect you and give you a place for your soul to grow to be strong enough one day to live and provide for your own this warmth in the immense meatlocker blackness of an ordinary world.

This however was the knowledge to come. All that you knew now was, when that heavy porcelain bone tinted china plate was set down in front of you your eyes filled as fast as your nose from the meal. The thick golden brown pile of french fries, the warmed bun cradling the steaming hamburger and you ate it all without looking up or saying a word.

When at last you were done you pushed the plate away and wiped your mouth with the big white paper napkin and crushed it into a ball and laid it on the middle of the plate and saw the green pickle and ate it too, despite that you really didn't like pickles.

When the counterman came over to clear the plates, he looked at you and said as he tilted his paper hat back on his forehead,

"I'll be dammed you ate the whole thing, not many of them eat the whole thing these days, when I was in the war I saw families who could live off a week over what gets wasted in here in one afternoon."

And when he returned with the check he had a Candy Cane in his hand for you.

Then it was back out in the cold grey street, holding her hand, following his foot steps as you were led though block after block of filthy slabs of concrete feeling full and a little sleepy. As the din of traffic roared all around, you could still hear the words of that man back there in white shaking your father's hand and saying, "I just don't know what ever happened to all the good little girls and boys."

Good night Hank. Good Night Frank. Good Night Jack.

11/30/94

THEM!

A fat little man with silver hair lies in a bed in a section 8 ward outside of Los Angeles. He's looking out the window at the city's canal system that handles sewer run-off. He's been watching for a long time. He's mumbling to himself, ma. . . ma . . . morning . . . morning in . . . Ammmer iiccaaa. America. The tubby little man with the silver hair looks a little like Oliver Hardy without the fuhrer's mustache.

Today is a big day for him. He has visitors. They crowd around his bed. They are a bunch of frightened people. They are terrified by a changing world. They believe that their way of life is being threatened. They believe that anyone who is different than they are is certainly dangerous. They believe that the little fat man with the silver hair in the bed by the window in the section 8 ward has the answers. He anxiously looks out the window at the empty concrete corridors and says, "It was THEM, they're gone. They were here. All of THEM . . . They'll be back."

The crowd around his bed looks nervous. They don't understand; young Jack Klugman from the Republican Twilight Zone where the monsters are due on Maple Street summons up enough courage to ask, "Anhh . . umm. So . . Newt what have you been up to???"
The little fat man pulls the sheet up over his head
 and starts kicking his feet while chanting,
"make me a sergeant, charge the booze, make me a sergeant
charge the booze." The assembled group stands puzzled.
Then he removes the sheet and with a knowing grin and
a hard glint in his eyes that shines with a brittle
razor smug sanity and answers the question,
"what have I been up to? . . 0. Nothing much,

BUT I Got PLANS!!!!!!!!
(for THEM!!!)"
There's a Contract out on America
There's a Contract out on America.

So bring on the huge black and white tap dancing mutant Ants for
the New Cocktail hour for those who just don't get it singing the
Newspeak of the opinion power elite,
  "The beatings will continue, until morale improves"
  "The beatings will continue, until morale improves"

Who is it that just isn't getting it?
The new THEM. Who are they? The short list includes;
Centralist/Liberal Christians moms with the pro-life
program, Media Jews, Secular Americans, working single women
with children, non-white Americans, gay and lesbians
tree-hugging environmentalists and all those pesky
intellectuals, artists and libertarians.
The new THEM will become the scapegoats for all the
serious problems afflicting American Society.
Men are back. Tough angry old white men.

The men that sport colognes called Brut.
And they will take a pass on poetry.
Big is back. Big gun. Big dick. Big Fun.
It's Big Dick Swinging and his Inquisition Orchestra.
But that doesn't mean music..... No more music, lyricism,
melody or wit.
More dissonance, insolence, arrogant shit.
Compassion is out. Sympathy is a weakness.
The soundtrack of contemporary society is the lynch mob
backbeat of an endless monotonous goose stepping
misanthropic lock-heel jack-boot march of hate.

Hate is cool. Hate is strength. Hate is the new big thing.

Hate Washington, Hate the president. Hate his wife.
Hate the Media. Hate the liberals. Hate the poor.
Hate the Bill of Rights. Hate Democracy.

But. Love. Love America.
The new democracy without rights.
The spokesman is "the see I told you so" man,
Gush Limburger. . And as you look at that cruel, mocking
pork pile you wonder why do the opening themes of Entertainment
Tonight, 700 Club and Sports Center all sound the same?

Meanwhile mean and stupid are having a race.
Every day it's just more mean and stupid. Neck and neck.
In the papers, on the random in your face.
There are no more standards, nothing left to disgrace,
because mean and stupid are having a race.

That's right. Every day it's just a little more mean
and stupid.
Big brother's cruelty and ignorance didn't even feel
it was a challenge. So they sent their little brothers.
Just a little mean and stupid is more than enough.

And it's the invasion of the Duracell people.
Nuclear Family? Nah. The battery acid family.
The Coppertop people.
They just moved in to your neighborhood on the left.
The Puttermans are here.
Almost human, mostly plastic, empowered by the right
kind of power, having the best smirking lines as their
hapless fellow citizens fall over in disgrace from having
the "wrong" points of view, suspect personal habits or
preferences, and of course the greatest debilitator...
just not enough of the "right" kind of power.
Cash $$$$$Dollars$$$$$

Bucks $$$$$Dead Presidents.
The "right" kind of thinking.
People who are poor....deserve to be.
People like that...are lazy.

People who are ugly....are stupid and useless.
The welcome wagon is coming.
Why it's the Borg. They brought Hugh with them.
Data's evil twin of purpose gave them permission
to think anew.
"Individuality is irrelevant."
All will be assimilated.
"Your humanity is irrelevant."
All will be assimilated.
"Cruel television reality will redefine your life."
All will be syndicated.

You will shop, snub, consume to excess, fear,
sneer, distrust, mainline credit cards and dismiss
everything that is not
an instantly gratifying Big Dick Swinging Ferry boat ride
to the Nation of plenty. Whether God is sitting in the
Mall like Santa, waiting for you to crawl on the Deity's
lap and whine for the rest of infinity, "I want....I
Want." I want.....want those BAD people to disappear.

Who are the new "bad" people?
Why...of course.......it's THEM.
They did it. They ruined the neighborhood.
Those with the funny, unpronounceable last names.
        They turned Bedford Falls into Pottersville.
They drive old cars. They smell funny.

But here comes the Hardcopy final solution.
It's.....it's....here comes Newty...like a ghost rider

on plush black velvet with sparkly high lights
who's that he has with him?
Why it's the ghost of Reagan...no....that's
Nixon....no....it's the evil Robert Dole
sharpening his eyebrows with a file.

Our next president William Blake's
"Old Nobodydaddy" complete with an erect: "Mannerstaat."
The big ants are back.
They're playing Roller Ball and doing Nike endorsements.
They wanted a culture war.
But they couldn't find any.
The looked and looked
In the end out of pure frustrations...they found THEM.
It was all their fault. THEM.
(All outta communists?)
No sweat, use THEM. (Fresh outta jews)
ssss.....o.k. use new improved all purpose THEM!
You're not one of THEM are you?
You don't think like THEM do you?
None of THEM are your friends...are they?
If we asked you to, would you turn THEM
over to us....wouldn't you?
Get THEM. Get THEM before it's too LATE!!!!

                                                    3/95

LIST OF THE END OF JANUARY

Snow coal cone lump ashtray pustule
shrinking in the corner of the parking lot.
(Ah....early spring)

Sound of clogged carburetor gagging on itself.
(Great...now you've flooded it)

Lost key trunk eyehole with yellow handle
long neck Phillip's screwdriver protruding.
(Nope that didn't work either...keep swearing)

False dawn slapping wind gagging away
slamming cheap tin bed frame freight train
ready to orgasm and derail.

Centipede shadow crawling measuring spoons
scurrying across the dingy white moon soaked linoleum floor
looking like a pool of quicksand.

Brown plastic garbage can rolling down the block
yawning in the gutter.

Air raid siren blast exploding
in a razor blade cable running through your ears
jerking your head off the sound sleep pillow.
(This was only a test)

Child's dream speak night talk back lit in
orange dragon space heater steel teeth
hissing at the bars on the crib.
(Some childhood memories are best forgotten.)

Fresh creme of the New Year
curdling in the calendar's carton.
(Whose face is that on the side?")

                                                    1/89

VANISHING BREED

The sound of the sirens
in the fog
woke you didn't it?

You're left wondering what
was on the other side
of the window.
Could it be the lessons of Gorgo?

So the deeper you go in the sheets,
the better you can recall
your last slow motion dream
where the waiters uniforms
smelt of perspiration and suicide.
The dishes breaking in their eyes.

Jack Sterling on the radio
that sat atop the refrigerator
at six thirty on
a Tuesday morning in 1964.
You swung your legs
waiting for him to finish
scrambling the eggs.

Spatula in one hand
cast iron frying pan in the other,
he said,
"So, the Naugahyde armrest slashed rubicund
and was repaired with scotch tape."

The shadow in the chair sat
pounding a pale bloody Mary,
waiting for the applause to die down.

"You know how it is with some people,
they think they can drink,
and the next thing you know
they're burying a steak knife
into the furniture.
They want to tell you about the lessons of Gorgo."

They are a vanishing breed.
The REM graduate and the dropout from clown college
sharing their apartment with a shaggy mutt
who is always attentive,
a parrot that lisps,
the monkey named Stanley,
who can dance a gig and beg for quarters,
and don't forget that mangy rabbit
confined to a dirty, newsprint cage.

They move from room to room
with a kind of slim, lean hip devotion.

He didn't believe in handing out tickets.
He preferred bawling them out.
He said, "they'll remember THAT better."

So now he sat dejected in a corner
nursing a drink
waiting for the applause to die down.
Thinking from the Latin, "applauder"
waiting to explode.

90

RUBBER EDEN

He liked to drink the coffee
from a smooth stone cup
in a wide booth, up in the front.
Off the windows where rode ambient chatter
where a door rang a bell hooked to
a sensor beam that
sliced up the legs and ankles
of everyone's entrances and exits

Here in the Rubber Eden.

He liked to think he lived in a time
of complete image castration.
All was category.
Category was all.
One's behavior received a unit code.
Every action begged workshop.
A point of view was good for a laugh or a jail sentence.
All protest was negative.
All consumption was positive.
All excess was a blot on the face of a nation
choking down abstinence
like a bulemic in Dunkin' Donuts.

He liked to smoke and have a face full
of warnings and threats.
Deadly mundane combinations were his "forte."
He contradicted himself regularly
and berated his closest friends endlessly.
At the moment he was taking a swing
at the waitress.

Just a nice guy
having a nice meal
in Perkins.

He liked to stare at his own reflection
in the window and drink the coffee
from a smooth stone cup.

Here in the Rubber Eden.

1/89